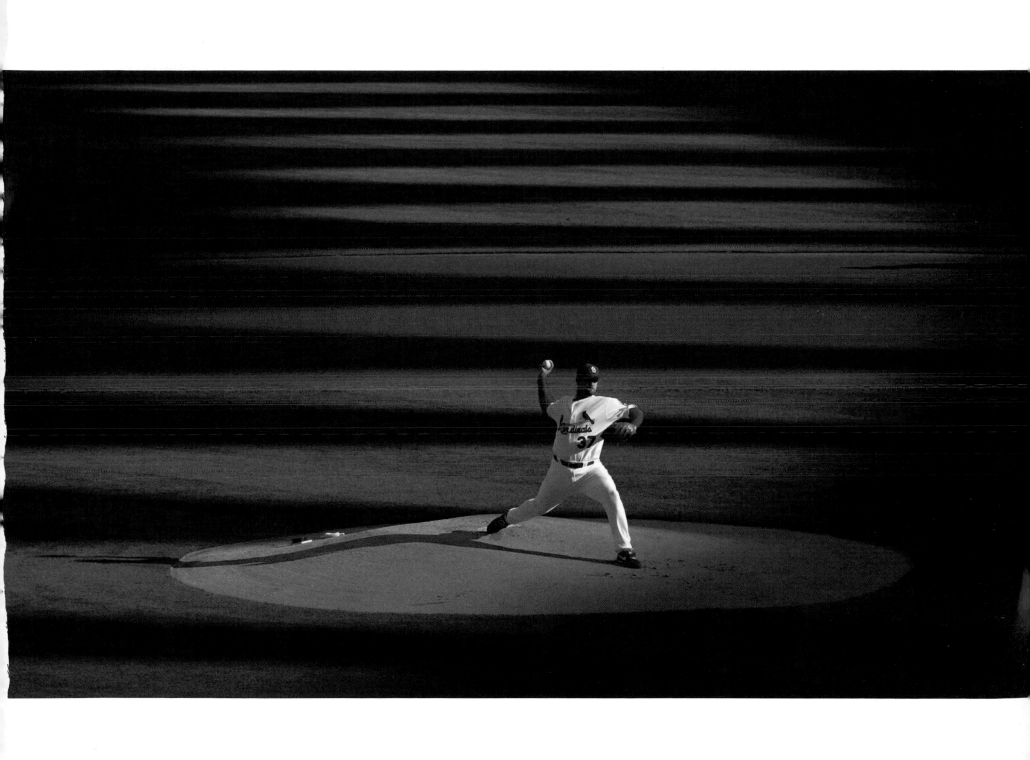

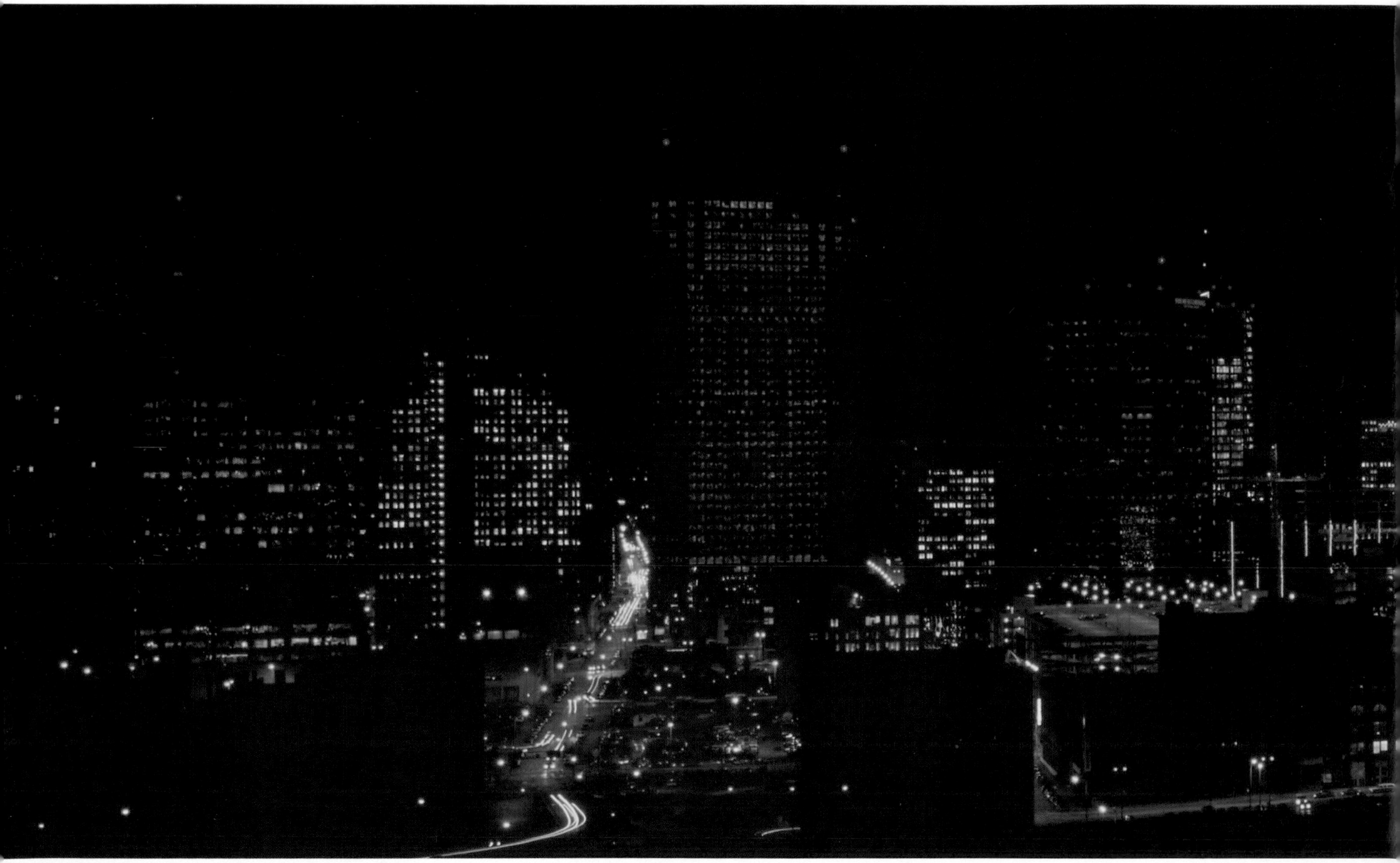

BUSCH STADIUM MOMENTS

BUSCH STADIUM MOMENTS

Editor
Mike Smith

Art Direction / Design
Christine Reynolds Zueck

Photo Editor
Larry Coyne

Author
Dan O'Neill

Copy Editor
Ron Cobb

Contributing writers
Joe Buck, Robert W. Duffy, Bernie Miklasz

Contributing copy editors
Curtis Peck, Marsha Sanguinette

Assistant photo editor
Hillary Levin

Busch Stadium research
Mark D. Learman

St. Louis timeline research
J. Stephen Bolhafner

Sales and marketing
John Maher, Nancy Long

Special thanks to Doug Weaver of Kansas City
Star Books, and to the St. Louis Cardinals.

Hardcover:
ISBN-10: 0-9661397-2-0
ISBN-13: 978-0-9661397-2-3

Leatherbound:
ISBN-10: 0-9661397-3-9
ISBN-13: 978-0-9661397-3-0

Printed by Walsworth Publishing Co., Marceline, Mo.

To order additional copies, call 800-329-0224.
Order online at www.STLtoday.com/buschbook

CONTENTS

302

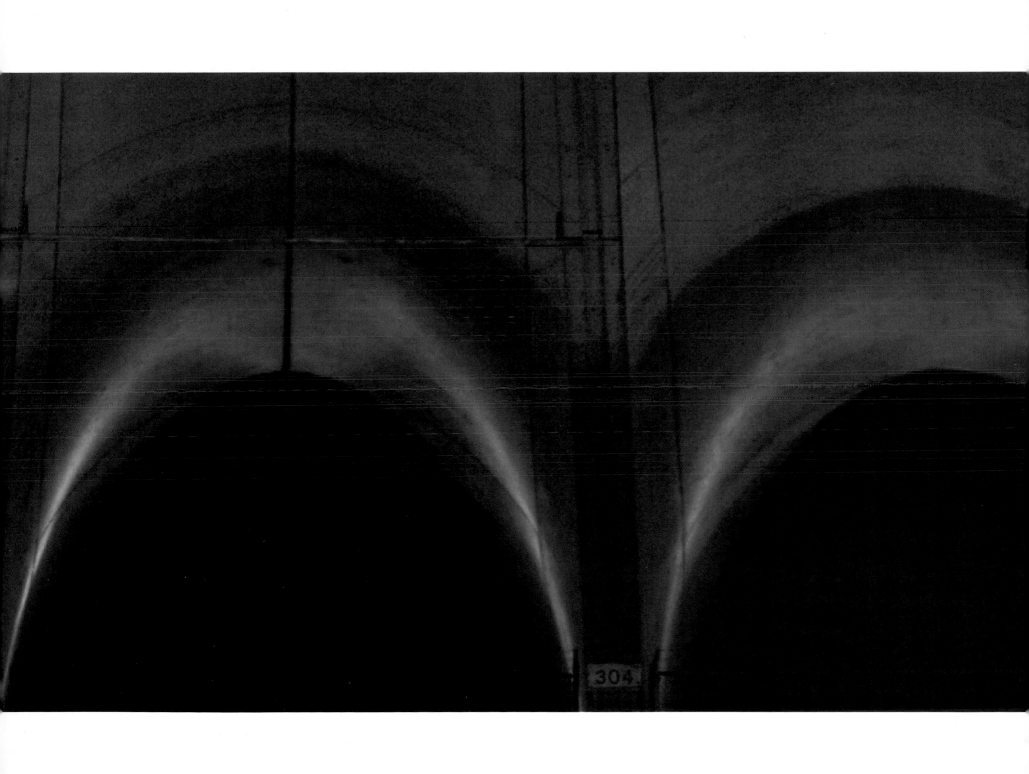

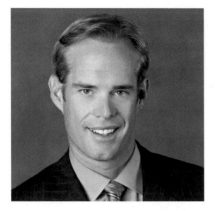

Joe Buck

Maybe for the first time

in my professional life, I am the perfect man for the job.

If this book deals with the total history of Busch Stadium, not just the Cardinals, then who better to write this than someone who literally grew up within its friendly confines?

Anyone who reads this probably has at least a handful of stories about Busch that will stay with them for the rest of their lives. I don't have many life stories — period — that don't in some small way involve that ballpark. The stadium was built by the brewery in 1966. I was built by Jack and Carole Buck in 1969, and from that point forward Busch Stadium and I have been inseparable.

I was a lucky kid. My father, who came to St. Louis in 1954 and worked in the park from the moment it opened until he passed away, always wanted me with him. My earliest childhood memories are of baseball, the Cardinals and the KMOX radio booth.

When I was 4 years old, I had a moment I will never forget. In the KMOX booth, there was a lower level where the broadcasters worked, and a seating area five steps above that looked out at the field and down on those calling the action. One afternoon I was sitting up in that area with my mom watching the game while I drank a Coke. In a moment of sheer bliss during a Cardinals rally — I think Ted Simmons got a big hit — I knocked over the soda onto the broadcasters below. Spinning around, Jack Buck and Mike Shannon gave looks that made this fragile little guy burst into tears. They had no idea when they turned around that I, the little fat kid, had done it. They had to spend the rest of the hot, humid afternoon sticky with my soda all over their 1970s clothes, and I had to spend the rest of the week convincing

myself that it was indeed safe to enter the booth again before I turned 11. Dr. Phil might be amazed that even with that traumatic experience, I would someday share that booth with my father and Mike as a Cardinals announcer.

I won't bore you with specific stories about my life at Busch, but I do think it is fun — as it probably is for you — to recount things that I witnessed and participated in there. I spent night after night in the ballpark and missed PLENTY of school because of late nights downtown with the Cardinals. The cool thing was that my parents wanted me there.

From those days as a 4-year-old to the nights spent waiting for my dad to finish work while I hit tennis balls and Wiffleballs against a wall with John Simmons, Ted's son, in the hallway outside the Cardinals clubhouse, life was great at Busch. I learned the game there, listening to my dad and Mike and hanging around players such as Keith Hernandez, Tony Scott and Jerry Mumphrey. I learned how to pitch under the watchful eye of Hub Kittle, Whitey's pitching coach, in the Cardinals' bullpen. I got to meet star players by tagging around after my father while he went into the visitors' clubhouse to introduce himself to the fresh-faced call-ups who were visiting Busch Stadium for the first time.

I also got to meet a lot of you, I'm sure, while literally clinging to my father's coattails and holding his beer as he signed autographs after games.

My memories of the stadium, like yours, do not just involve baseball. There are plenty of football moments as well. Even winning football moments for me. I played in a state championship game at Busch for Country Day School. I will never forget the feeling of running out onto that field for my own game. It was overwhelming, and miraculously I did not trip. It felt as if we were playing in my back yard, and even though I played sparingly, the one or two tackles I made are still on my personal sports highlight reel.

In 1985, as a frequent visitor in the KMOX booth at Busch Stadium, 16-year-old Joe Buck needs to look no farther for a role model than his father, Hall of Fame broadcaster Jack Buck.

I saw a U2 concert there ... the Shriners circus ... watched Big Mac hit historic home run No. 62 from my broadcast booth, just next to my father's. I witnessed Cardinals fans streaming onto the field after Bruce Sutter struck out Gorman Thomas to end the 1982 World Series. At age 15, I went on my first date with the woman who is now my wife and got hit on the knee by a Terry Pendleton foul ball.

When I was 20 years old, I got to sit in the best seat in the house and call my first baseball game on KMOX. I shared the microphone with my father and Mike as I broadcast a Cardinals-Phillies game. For 11 years I was able to call my dad my partner there, which I had always felt he was anyway. My career as well as my life was shaped at Busch.

I was in the seats when my father was honored by the fans and the team after his enshrinement in baseball's Hall of Fame in 1987. I was there when St. Louisans and baseball fans across America ventured out again after 9/11. I watched with tears in my eyes as my dad delivered his poem about the tragedy and how strong this nation has always been.

I stood behind home plate with my wife and children the day after my father died and tried as best as I could not to cry as we all said goodbye to a man who meant so much to so many.

Busch Stadium has really been my second home almost since the day I was born. It has been my playroom, my office and my family's place of mourning. The sight of it has always brought a smile to my face. I will never forget the feeling I got as a homesick college freshman at Indiana University during the 1987 World Series. I sat in my dorm room, crushed, ready to give all $90 I had in the bank to be there.

Driving home on school breaks, I knew when I saw that stadium I was home. If the lights were on and the team was in town, I'd pull right off and run in to hug my dad and watch my Cardinals.

So much has happened there, it is a shame Busch had to come down. But the team needed a new stadium. All across the major leagues, new ballparks are popping up. If there is one in Houston and Cincinnati and Pittsburgh, in my mind, there should be one in our town. Cardinals fans deserve the best, and I honestly believe this new field will give the team more revenue to put back into the roster.

If it makes any difference to you, my father was in favor of a new stadium as well. He couldn't wait to see the plans for what would have been his third Busch Stadium.

I am going on only my second. When it came down, it was a punch to the gut, an emotional moment for me. I am not big on making inanimate objects sound human, but I will say this: For as long as I can remember, it has been a great friend. I am so glad my children got to watch and learn how special Cardinals baseball is there. I can only hope their kids have the same type of memories in the new park.

They will — that's how these things work. You grow up and move on. The tough part here is that unlike that childhood home you used to live in and always want to visit so you can see what the new owners have done to your old room, this building came down. This special place will have to continue on in our memories and stories. Three generations of Bucks have felt at home at Busch Stadium.

Like many of you, we will miss it.

I dedicate this piece to Mattie Lott, the longtime Busch Stadium elevator operator, who was so sweet to all the Bucks, and who also is missed.

Joe Buck and his father, Jack, call a Cardinals game in 1996. The KMOX booth at Busch Stadium was Joe's home away from home since early childhood.

The birth of Busch

BY ROBERT DUFFY OF THE POST-DISPATCH

The late, great Busch Memorial Stadium in downtown St. Louis was by anyone's estimation a glorious building, and was the kind of building any good architect hopes to achieve. It was a deft combination of a pressing, practical need, a sense of history and high-minded ideals of civic responsibility. Instantly, it was recognized as more than a stadium. It was a building of national consequence. Over the years, as it admirably performed its work, it more than earned its keep as a functional machine for sport and as a symbol of the city of St. Louis. It could have served the former purpose without its graceful crown of arches, a rhythmic procession of forms that made subtle reference to the shape of architect Eero Saarinen's monumental sculpture, the Gateway Arch, and without its modernist colonnade of steel uprights that gave the building support and transparency. But the 1966 Busch Stadium came close, in fact, to being just another big cookie cutter rather like the 2006 stadium will be a restatement of what began as a fresh idea in Oriole Park at Camden Yards in Baltimore in 1992.

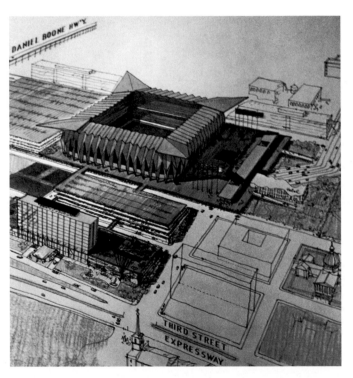

By the late 1950s, plans for a new stadium are taking shape. Proposals for the stadium's design include this one in 1958.

RIGHT: In the early 1960s, as the Gateway Arch begins to rise in the distance, the downtown neighborhood known as Chinatown occupies an area bounded roughly by Market, Walnut, Seventh and Eighth streets. Chinatown would be torn down to make room for construction of the new stadium and adjacent parking lots.

MOMENTS

"The people of St. Louis have shown they are really big league. For our part, we intend to keep up St. Louis' reputation as a major league city."

— Stan Musial, sending congratulations from spring training in 1962 after voters approved a bond issue that was key to building a downtown stadium.

But the razed Busch Stadium, now in the company of so many other treasures laid to waste and then to rest in a rather distinguished architectural graveyard, was born at a moment when the owner of the baseball team, August A. Busch Jr., and St. Louis' civic establishment understood that form and function in careful balance are fundamental elements of a brilliant and durable marriage.

In mid-20th-century major league history and the midcentury life of St. Louis, there was the need for something better and new in the sports stadium department. Bing Devine, who served twice as vice president and general manager of the Cardinals (from 1958 to 1964 and again from 1968 to 1978), said that although one might debate the wisdom of building a new stadium for 2006, there was no question that the old ballpark at Grand and Dodier had had it.

Not only was there cause to move from the old Busch Stadium for baseball, but there was also need for a stadium that would accommodate professional football. Joseph Griesedieck, president of the Falstaff Brewing Co., wanted to bring the Chicago Cardinals to St. Louis. A new downtown stadium was key to the success of his negotiations, he claimed.

But another need, less easily quantified, was communal — to express civic substance and muscle and sophistication in architecture, an impulse that has been repeated continually since human beings first moved from caves and lean-tos and huts, and as a means of reviving the city's core.

The metaphor of sport can be applied to this desire. Building great buildings is a competition, a way for a man or a city or a nation to say with steel and brick and stone and concrete, and with

Excavation for the stadium was under way by June 1964. This view looks south from Seventh Street, which had to be rerouted around the stadium.

shapes and forms that have formed a common visual vocabulary through the ages, "We have played the game and we have won."

All those complex, contradictory and competing impulses were as much a part of the structure of Busch Stadium as were its steel and concrete, bleachers and scoreboard, turf and bright lights.

RIGHT: In November 1962, principals in the birth of Busch Stadium gather as demolition began. From the right are Mayor Raymond R. Tucker; James P. Hickok, president of Civic Center Redevelopment Corp.; Charles L. Farris, executive director of the Land Clearance for Redevelopment Authority; and Aloys P. Kaufmann, president of the Chamber of Commerce.

The contract is signed for construction of the stadium and a 2,800-car parking garage. From left are O.O. McCracken, executive vice president of Civic Center Redevelopment Corp.; F.C. Ahrens, vice president of Fruin-Colnon Construction Co.; Preston Estep, chairman of Civic Center Redevelopment's executive commission; and I.E. Millstone, president of Millstone Construction Inc.

It is humorous to look back and discover that the seed for a new stadium was planted not in the interests of professional baseball or football but for Washington University's Battling Bears, a respectable team perhaps — but not the sort of organization that would cause a community to set about to build a major sports facility.

When the "new" stadium opened in 1966, Post-Dispatch reporter Carl Baldwin wrote, "... the first proposal for a riverfront stadium in St. Louis apparently was made in 1935 when St. Louisans were beginning to realize again the important role the Mississippi River plays in the city's welfare."

Baldwin reported that Jimmy Conzelman, athletic director and football coach at Washington U., and the school's then chancellor, George Reeves Throop, had great ambitions for the Bears, envisioning their emerging from the hibernation of obscurity and into a league with Notre Dame and Army.

No great intelligence was required to see that good old Francis Field, beloved and historic as it may be, was not a suitable grid-iron for such august company. Conzelman and Throop proposed a riverfront stadium, recognizing that downtown was convenient to fans in Missouri and Illinois.

The Post-Dispatch's sports editor, John Edward Wray, also pumped the western shore of the Mississippi as a good place for sport. And in 1938, Mayor Bernard F. Dickmann made the initial official proposal for a 60,000-seat stadium downtown, to be a major element of the Jefferson National Expansion Memorial. That memorial would eventually emerge as Saarinen's Gateway Arch.

ST. LOUIS MOMENTS

1958
Local dreamer Bill Bangert envisions building a 100,000-seat domed stadium in the county. He hopes to attract the 1964 Olympics but goes bankrupt promoting the plan.

1959
A tornado rips through the city in February, killing 21, toppling the Channel 2 tower and tearing off part of The Arena's roof.

1960
U.S. Census Bureau reports that St. Louis has a population of 750,026, down more than 100,000 from 1950, the city's first population loss ever.

1961
Excavation begins for the foundation of the Gateway Arch, 28 years after the monument was first proposed.

Architect Edward Durell Stone (center) looks over his model of the stadium's exterior in March 1963. After original designs are deemed unworthy, civic leaders opt to bring in Stone from New York. His ring of 96 concrete arches along the stadium's rim becomes Busch's most distinctive feature.

1962

In a space capsule made in St. Louis by McDonnell Aircraft Corp., John Glenn becomes the first American to orbit Earth.

1963

A seven-month parade of demonstrations for equal employment opportunities at Jefferson Bank & Trust becomes the watershed for race relations in St. Louis.

1964

While St. Louis celebrates the city's Bicentennial, civil rights activist Percy Green climbs up one side of the incomplete Arch to protest a lack of minority contractors.

1965

Gateway Arch is topped out Oct. 28 — but not before fire department pumpers spray water to cool the steel in the south leg, which is warped by hot weather.

As Baldwin noted, even though the war years intervened, the complementary ideas of a stadium and civic improvement did not evaporate. And when the war was done, peacetime maneuvers were initiated in the hope of building a new downtown stadium.

A stalwart standard-bearer of the new stadium was Washington University alumnus A. Carl Weber, a member of the Quarterback Club and a vice president of Laclede Steel. The Post-Dispatch's Baldwin said Weber gave more than a hundred speeches on the subject between 1945 and 1956 to just about anyone who'd listen: garden clubs, war groups, service organizations.

By this time, the Jefferson National Expansion Memorial and the stadium had become independent. Charles L. Farris, who, for good or ill, was the dynamic proprietor of the St. Louis Land Clearance for Redevelopment Authority and an evangelist for urban renewal, presented a proposal in 1958 that gave, as Baldwin said, "form and substance to Busch Memorial Stadium."

Farris' plan called for a $30 million stadium on 71 acres between Third, Seventh, Market and Walnut streets. It was submitted to what was then called the Chamber of Commerce. Led by the legendary banker James P. Hickok, president of the region's bluest-chip bank, First National, the gears of St. Louis' financial and commercial transmission were engaged, and in 1959, with the creation of the Civic Center Redevelopment Corp., the engine of progress moved steadily ahead.

A $5 million pledge from Anheuser-Busch to be incorporated into $20 million in equity capital to guarantee a loan added steam and assured the baronial name of Busch would be forever attached to the new building.

The first girder for Busch Memorial Stadium rises in January 1965. At this point, the first baseball game to be played in the stadium is only 16 months away.

There were, of course, inevitable delays, derailments and adjustments. Architects are notorious narcissists; Saarinen fretted that a new stadium would "disbalance" the skyline. His objection was overruled. However, there was another objection on aesthetic grounds. It was sustained.

RIGHT: Workers survey the progress of Busch Stadium construction during a lunch break on a chilly March day in 1965.

build a multimillion-dollar stadium without involving a great architect in its design.

Hickok argued he had one — the formidable Gen. Leif J. Sverdrup, head of the Sverdrup & Parcel engineering company. Baer told Hickok, "He's an engineer, not an architect. He's really got you bamboozled."

Baer set his standards internationally high, recommending Pier Luigi Nervi, the Italian virtuoso of stadium design. Recognizing that snaring Nervi might be too grand a dream, Baer told Hickok there were other architects, American architects, who could turn out a functional building the community could embrace with pride, unlike the middling proposal advanced by Sverdrup and his local associates.

The conflict between Baer and Sverdrup was head-to-head and bitter, but when Gussie Busch decided he did not want his, his children's and his grandchildren's name on an ugly building, Howard Baer's insistence that a building as important as Busch Stadium must be visually satisfying as well as functional prevailed.

Architect Edward Durell Stone was engaged to design the exterior of the building, and a more sculptural Busch Stadium was the result. The Post-Dispatch's distinguished art and architecture critic George McCue wrote, "In his design, Stone demonstrates that he has a dependable taste and a sensitiveness to what is appropriate for a river town on a historic site in the Middle West."

Stone's Busch Stadium was built in a flurry of optimism for renewal of downtown, but its building involved the razing of another myth-shrouded ballpark, the old Busch Stadium at Grand and Dodier, also known, maybe better known, as Sportsman's Park.

In December 1964, an aerial view shows Broadway on the right, running north toward the Old Courthouse, and Eighth Street on the far left.

Howard Baer was one of the great Renaissance characters of St. Louis. He read Greek and Roman classics in their original languages and understood intuitively that a citizenry deserved public buildings of architectural consequence.

He correctly judged the original architectural scheme for Busch Memorial Stadium to be deficient. In his memoir, "Saint Louis to Me," he recalled asking Hickok, "How stupid can you be?" to

---

RIGHT: In June 1965, progress is being made on construction of the stadium and the Gateway Arch. The Arch would be completed four months later.

MOMENTS

"The first thing I think about Busch Stadium is it saved downtown St. Louis. Everything else aside, it did an awful lot to clean up the city."

— Jack Buck,
Cardinals broadcaster

August A. Busch Jr. (left foreground) meets in his office in July 1965 with other civic leaders to discuss construction of the stadium. At an earlier meeting on the stadium, when early designs met with disapproval, Busch reportedly stood up and said, "I've got $5 million of Busch money in this thing. When my grandchildren walk around this town, they ought to be proud of it. Get an architect!"

The old ballpark, while beloved and a genuine vessel of sports history and civic congregation, had become obsolete.

Here's Bing Devine again:

"Sportsman's Park was really aged," he said. There was also the problem of parking, and fans often parked in the front yards of houses in the neighborhood. Devine said to add parking spaces, houses would have to be sacrificed.

"It was not only the age of the park but also the location, too."

On May 8, the character of that mythic location changed forever.

Post-Dispatch sportswriter Ed Wilks was there. He described how retired groundskeeper Bill Stocksick came onto the field wearing a white shirt, a necktie and a brown hat and dug up home plate.

"The digging ... came a few minutes after 3:15 p.m. yesterday. That's when shortstop Jim Davenport scooped up a ground ball by Alex Johnson and flipped to second baseman Tito Fuentes, who pivoted and threw to first baseman Orlando Cepeda for a close-out double play that finished the Cardinals' final game at Busch Stadium." The Cardinals lost to the Giants 10-5.

Sure there was nostalgia, Wilks said, and he etched the bitter-sweetness of the moment.

"There was a parade then, and a ride downtown. And there was a new scoreboard to watch and messages, in color. And bands and singers and fireworks.

"The new stadium was in the spotlight now. ... and at Grand and Dodier, the Old Lady just stood there." ■

RIGHT: "In substance, (Busch Memorial Stadium) probably is more magnificent than envisioned in any dream because no lay dreamer could have imagined the final monumental design, the brilliant scalloped canopy and the delicacy of the slender piers. It took inspired architects to do that." — from a Post-Dispatch editorial in spring 1966.

The 1960s

BY DAN O'NEILL OF THE POST-DISPATCH

And so they built it, and so they came. In the midst of a dynamic decade of cultural and social transformation, St. Louis embarked on a profound new era of civic enlightenment with the opening of Civic Center Busch Memorial Stadium. Slightly controversial for those who debated its purpose, slightly tardy for the baseball season opener, and still slightly rough around the edges, the expansive downtown facility opened its gates to the sporting public on May 12, 1966. The inauguration proved appropriately exciting and successful. The Cardinals beat the Atlanta Braves 4-3 in 12 innings, with Hall of Famer Lou Brock hitting a game-winning single off Hall of Famer Phil Niekro. For the record, and for future trivia arguments, Cardinals righthander Ray Washburn threw the first pitch (ball one) at 8:04 p.m., Atlanta's Gary Geiger had the first hit (single to right), hometown favorite Mike Shannon had the first run batted in (run-scoring triple), Atlanta's Felipe Alou had the first home run, Hall of Fame pitcher Bob Gibson had the first pinch-hit (a single) and Cardinals infielder Jimy Williams (later a big-league manager) offered up the first good quip about Busch: "You could put my whole

In the minds of many Cardinals fans, a high point of the 1960s is Bob Gibson's performance on Oct. 2, 1968, when he sets a World Series record with 17 strikeouts against the Detroit Tigers at Busch Stadium.

MOMENTS

"I've never seen major-league hitters overmatched that way. It was like watching a big-league pitcher against Little League batters. It was frightening."

— Mike Shannon, who played third base when Bob Gibson struck out 17 Detroit Tigers in Game 1 of the 1968 World Series at Busch Stadium

"I've been playing baseball since I was 7 years old. But when Gibby closed in on that record, it was the first time in my life I had chills run up and down my spine."

— Dal Maxvill, who played shortstop that day

33

hometown in here," said Williams, from Arroyo Grande, Calif. "In fact, you could put the whole town on the pitcher's mound."

With 96 open arches swirling along its rim, the concrete wonder was designed to complement the new Gateway Arch – which had been completed the previous October. Simplistic and spacious, Busch Memorial seduced its awe-struck audiences with wide chairs, electronic message boards, an automated infield tarp and unobstructed views. For those accustomed to views obstructed by steel support beams, rickety wooden seats and antiquated amenities on Grand Boulevard, it was a whole new ballgame.

Old Busch Stadium had once been known as Sportsman's Park. New Busch Stadium promised to be Sportsman's Paradise.

The 1966 season proved uneventful baseball-wise, with the Cardinals finishing 12 games out of first. But the maiden voyage for the downtown showground was marked by momentous events. On July 12, Busch Memorial played host to baseball's All-Star Game — the only time the spectacle was staged there. The largest crowd to attend a sports event in St. Louis to that point— 49,936 — poured in for a Mid-Summer Classic that turned into a Mid-Summer Sweatshop. As the mercury rose to 103 degrees, salt tablets and oxygen replaced hot dogs and soda pop as the condiments of choice.

The game went extra innings and provided extra dramatics when Cardinals catcher Tim McCarver scored the winning run for the National League in the 10th. Perhaps the most vivid memory of the day, however, was a comment by NL honorary coach Casey Stengel.

In the 1960s, broadcaster Harry Caray and the Cardinals are virtually synonymous. Both a cheerleader and a critic, Caray enthralls listeners with his signature calls of "Holy cow!" and "It might be, it could be, it is … a home run!" The native St. Louisan's 25-year association with the ballclub comes to an unceremonious end with his firing after the 1969 season.

ST. LOUIS MOMENTS

1966

Sizzling July temperatures coupled with the rising popularity of air conditioning so taxes the Union Electric Co. that St. Louis neighborhoods take turns enduring power blackouts. The heat wave is blamed for 146 deaths.

1967

Ben Kerner puts the city's NBA team, the Hawks, up for sale in January. Nine months later, the Blues begin play as the city's National Hockey League team.

Pitcher Steve Carlton signs autographs at Busch Stadium on April 7, 1969. Oddly enough, "Lefty" was righthanded when it came to signing his name.

St. Louis is spared any street rioting in the aftermath of Dr. Martin Luther King Jr.'s murder. Instead, a peaceful mass march to honor his memory begins with 7,000 people at the Arch and swells to more than 35,000 marchers by the time it reaches Forest Park.

Mayor Alfonso J. Cervantes brings a replica of the Santa Maria to the St. Louis riverfront from New York, where it had been displayed at the 1964 World's Fair. But the boat is crushed by the Becky Thatcher after the vessels are torn from their mooring in a storm.

Undeterred by the rain at Busch Stadium, a couple of fans express their enthusiasm for the Beatles at a concert on Aug. 21, 1966. A crowd of 23,143 saw four other acts that evening, but only the Beatles create the kind of hyperventilation that results in trips to the first-aid station. "It's mild hysteria," a nurse said. "The symptoms are weeping, wailing and uncontrollable shaking. I tell them to sit down and cool off."

When asked what he thought of the new ballpark, the venerable "Perfesser" offered: "This new park sure holds the heat well. It took the press right out of my pants."

Later that summer, on Aug. 21, another Kodak keepsake took place when the Beatles played at the stadium. A crowd of Fab Four fanatics sat through a rainy evening to experience "Beatlemania" firsthand, including the usual complement of shrieking, fainting teenage girls.

The football Cardinals moved into their new digs on Sept. 11 with a 16-13 victory over the Philadelphia Eagles, as Jim Bakken kicked the winning field goal with five seconds remaining.

The ensuing years in the 1960s provided many more magical moments as the stadium settled into the St. Louis landscape. The St. Louis Stars, charter members of the new North American Soccer League, took up residency in 1967. A year later, the Stars played host to Santos of Brazil and the world's pre-eminent athlete — Pele.

Dan Devine's Missouri Tigers made a stop at Busch, pummeling Illinois in 1969 on their road to the Orange Bowl.

But the defining moments of the decade were provided by the Cardinals, who officially sanctioned the new "Field of Dreams" with back-to-back World Series appearances in 1967 and 1968. The '67 edition streaked to 101 wins and the NL pennant, led by the MVP numbers and nudging of Orlando "Cha-Cha" Cepeda. "El Birdos" beat the Boston Red Sox in the Fall Classic, doing so in classic, seven-game style.

The following year belonged to pitcher Bob Gibson, who stamped his Hall of Fame ticket with historic performances during the regular season and the postseason.

The decade came to a close without more world championships, but the novice ballpark had sown its oats, and a vibrant new piece of St. Louis sports culture was firmly entrenched. ■

In December 1967, patrons in the Stadium Club follow the action in a Cardinals football game, with their images reflected in the club's windows. At a time before luxury suites at stadiums were commonplace, the private restaurant at the Stadium Club was the ultimate in high-class spectating.

A grand opening

May 1966

The move to the riverfront agreed with River City baseball fans from the start. On May 8, 1966, St. Louis closed the book on a 46-year run of Cardinals baseball at Grand and Dodier with a loss to the San Francisco Giants. On May 12, 1966, Lou Brock singled off Phil Niekro in the 12th inning, opening the new book of baseball at Stadium Plaza with a victory. The first game at Busch Memorial Stadium also gave St. Louisans a first gander at their new first baseman. The Giants had traded slugger Orlando Cepeda to the Cardinals moments after that final game at old Busch Stadium, and Cepeda made his home debut along with the new facility. Ultimately, the Cardinals' first season in their new nest proved unremarkable. The club was 39-43 and 12 1/2 games out of first place by the time the Mid-Summer Classic arrived, and it never got within serious striking distance. The final ledger, 83-79 and sixth place, was a competitive push. But the signs of things to come were unmistakable. Lou Brock stole 74 bases, Bob Gibson won 21 games and the new guy, Cepeda, batted .303 and was named the NL Comeback Player of the Year. Those three Hall of Famers would be instrumental in Busch's unforgettable Summer of '67. ■

On May 8, 1966, retired groundskeeper Bill Stocksick hands over home plate to be delivered by helicopter from the old ballpark at Grand and Dodier to the new stadium downtown.

RIGHT: Cardinals owner August A. Busch Jr., second from left, is among the dignitaries at a parade marking the dedication of the new stadium. To the right of Busch are Mayor Alfonso J. Cervantes and his wife, Carmen; Gov. Warren E. Hearnes; Rep. Leonor Sullivan; Lt. Gov. Thomas Eagleton and County Supervisor Lawrence Roos.

MOMENTS

"I remember sitting with my son in the ballpark years later. I told him, 'You know, your dad was the first player to cross home plate here.'

"That's something nobody will ever be able to take away from me."

— St. Louisan Jerry Buchek, who grew up to play for the Cardinals and scored the first run at Busch Stadium

On May 12, 1966, while the Cardinals warm up before the first game played at Busch Stadium, a helicopter descends (above the scoreboard) to deliver the American flag.

The city's sparkling new stadium is all aglow for its debut on May 12, 1966. The crowd of 46,048, at the time the largest to see a baseball game in Missouri, includes former Cardinal Ray Blades, who had played in old Busch Stadium more than 40 years earlier. From his seat in the upper deck, he said, "Just came down to see how things were being run. Fifteen more feet up and I'd be in heaven."

All-Star sizzler

July 12, 1966

The highlight of the first baseball season at Busch Stadium — or perhaps the lowlight for fans who sat in the sun — occurred during a July heat wave when the All-Star Game came to town. Almost 50,000 fans began pouring through the gates at 1 p.m., eager to get a glimpse of the game's elite. Few regular-season games were televised at the time, so the opportunity to watch American League stars such as Al Kaline, Frank Robinson and Harmon Killebrew was especially intriguing. The pitching matchup was first-rate: Sandy Koufax vs. Denny McLain. The National League lineup included an outfield of Willie Mays, Hank Aaron and Roberto Clemente. Vice President Hubert H. Humphrey threw out the first ball. What those who attended would remember most about the day, however, was the heat — and we're not talking about fastballs. On a humid, sunny day, the temperature officially topped out at 103 degrees, but reportedly went as high as 105. While Baltimore Orioles star Brooks Robinson was treated to the MVP trophy, more than 50 spectators were treated for heat exhaustion. "It wasn't just that the heat was hot," said Bing Devine, who was general manager of the New York Mets in 1966. "The seats were hot. Too hot to sit on. If it had been on artificial turf, it might have been impossible to play the game." ∎

MOMENTS

"I'll give you an idea how hot it was out there: When Koufax started pitching for us, I began hollering, 'C'mon, Sanford.' Then I yelled, 'C'mon, Sandy.' And then, 'C'mon, Sand.' It was only the second inning, but it got too hot to holler, so I quit."

**— Joe Torre,
starting catcher for the
National League in the 1966
All-Star Game at Busch**

New York Mets skipper Casey Stengel serves as an honorary coach for the National League in the 1966 All-Star Game at Busch Stadium. On a day when the temperature hits 103 degrees, Stengel utters his famous backhanded compliment, "This new park sure holds the heat well."

RIGHT: Fans stake out spots on the sidewalk outside Busch Stadium, ready to wait overnight to buy standing-room tickets for the 1966 All-Star Game.

MOMENTS

"We had spent most of the All-Star Game in the bathroom, applying wet towels and just pouring water over our heads. But at one point I realized my parents had disappeared. An usher finally told me where they had been taken — my mother had fainted from the heat.

"Later that year, a doctor friend gave my mom a copy of the AMA's Journal. There was her picture: she was laying on a stretcher (soaking wet and white as a sheet) with my father leaning over her. The caption read: This woman was one of the many spectators affected by the heat at the All-Star Game in St. Louis."

— St. Louisan
Peggy Dubinsky Price

Vice President Hubert H. Humphrey greets American League batboy Jay Mazzone before the All-Star Game, with County Supervisor Lawrence Roos behind him. Humphrey had the honor of throwing out the game's first pitch.

The Cardinals' Tim McCarver slides home with the winning run in the bottom of the 10th inning in the All-Star Game, beating the throw from right fielder Tony Oliva to catcher Earl Battey. The umpire is Jim Honochick. McCarver scored from second base on a one-out single by Maury Wills for a 2-1 National League victory. "I felt I had to try to make them throw me out in that situation," McCarver said. "I was going all the way."

Fab Four fever

Aug. 21, 1966

MOMENTS

The Beatles said they didn't mind playing in the rain but were a bit apprehensive about possibly getting shocked by the wet electric amplifying equipment. But once on stage they grabbed the electric guitars and microphones fearlessly and attacked the music.

Thousands of fans screamed for the music, thousands got wet, hundreds were terribly upset by it all and a few dozen fainted.

— **Post-Dispatch review of the Beatles concert at Busch**

One of the most memorable nights in the almost-40-year history of Busch Memorial Stadium came just three months after it opened. On Aug. 21, 1966, the British Invasion reached the shores of the Mississippi River when the Beatles played at the new, $26 million facility. The stop was part of their third and final American tour. The appearance also came soon after John Lennon's comments about the group being more popular than Jesus, which fab-floored American audiences, particularly in the South. The furor had record stations banning Beatles music, churches sponsoring record burnings and troubled fans renouncing the Lads from Liverpool. By the time John, Paul, George and Ringo arrived in St. Louis — they played a concert in Cincinnati earlier the same day — the remnants of the controversy were still smoldering. In his Busch Stadium dressing room before the Sunday night concert, Paul McCartney had to address the backlash with reporters. But theology took a back seat to meteorology once the amps were plugged in. While tickets were $5 and $5.50, incredibly modest by today's standards, nasty weather put a damper on things, literally and figuratively. A crowd of 23,143 suffered the elements to see the show, which included five acts. Since the rain was expected to escalate as the evening progressed, the Beatles were moved up in the program, playing third in the batting order, ahead of the Ronettes and the Cyrkle. The mop tops performed 11 songs during a set that lasted 30 minutes. Meanwhile, business at the first-aid station was brisk. Nurses treated 35 girls for minor ailments, most common of which was diagnosed as "acute Beatlemania." ■

The Beatles have a mesmerizing effect on their fans in a concert at Busch Stadium. Later, the Beatles depart in two police cars, after police have to hold back some girls from jumping onto the cars.

The Beatles perform on a stage set up behind second base at the stadium, under a makeshift roof serving as protection from the rain. From left are George Harrison, Paul McCartney, Ringo Starr and John Lennon. Just moments earlier, they had dined on steaks in the lower level of the stadium, away from their adoring fans.

MOMENTS

"There was so much
excitement in the air, it was
almost too much to handle.
And then, there they were
— running across the field
carrying their guitars
and waving. The screams
overpowered the little
amps they had. I don't
recall being able to hear
a word (or note) they
were singing, but I just
remember the agony of
being so close, and yet
soooo far away from
John and Paul."

— St. Louisan Nancy Lewis

George Harrison and Ringo Starr in concert with the Beatles, for whom St. Louis was the 10th stop on a 14-city tour.

The many faces of Beatlemania — girls smitten by the Fab Four and, thankfully, restrained by the wire mesh behind home plate at Busch Stadium.

Bravo, bravo, El Birdos

Summer 1967

Orlando Cepeda became Cha-Cha the Cheerleader in 1967, turning into the vocal leader of "El Birdos." After many victories — including a doubleheader sweep of the Cubs — Cepeda jumped onto a box in the clubhouse and led cheers:

"We win two!"
Cha-Cha shouted.

"We win two!"
El Birdos shouted back.

"We're in first!"
Cha-Cha shouted.

"We're in first!"
El Birdos repeated.

— Post-Dispatch archives

Perhaps no summer at Busch Stadium was more enjoyable than the second summer, a summer of redemption, a summer of resilience, a summer of "El Birdos." The Cardinals took over first place in the National League on June 18, 1967, and never stalled, finishing 101-60 and 10½ games ahead of the pack. The cast included well-established characters such as Bob Gibson, Lou Brock, Julian Javier, Tim McCarver and Curt Flood. But perhaps the most compelling component was a transplant. Orlando Cepeda was branded as a malingerer in San Francisco, and on May 8, 1966, Cepeda was traded to the Cardinals. Embraced by his new teammates and fans, Cepeda found salvation and went on to be named the NL Comeback Player of the Year. In the Summer of '67, Cepeda further cemented the bond. His clubhouse clowning and unbridled enthusiasm made "Cha-Cha" the life of a season-long party in St. Louis, and he became the National League's first unanimous MVP choice since 1936. While Cepeda was reborn, his teammates were relentless. The litmus test came after July 15, when Gibson was struck by Roberto Clemente's smash and suffered a broken right leg. He would not make another start until Sept. 7. But in his absence, "El Birdos" kept on humming, and the Cardinals actually increased their first-place margin by 7½ games. In the World Series, the Cardinals faced the Red Sox, led by Jim Lonborg and Carl Yastrzemski. But Boston's "Impossible Dream" ran into St. Louis' "Unstoppable Duo" — Brock and Gibson. Brock batted .414, and Gibson returned to pitch three complete-game victories. "El Birdos" secured their place in Cardinals lore, and Busch Stadium secured its first world championship banner. ■

Bob Gibson collapses after being hit on the right shin by a liner off the bat of Roberto Clemente on July 15, 1967. Gibson gets up and faces three more batters before having to leave the game. The broken leg sidetracks Gibson but not the Cardinals.

The Cardinals' Lou Brock slides into third base with a triple in the first inning of Game 3 of the 1967 World Series at Busch Stadium. At left are Boston third baseman Dalton Jones and umpire Paul Pryor. Brock goes two for four and scores two runs in the Cardinals' 5-2 victory.

MOMENTS

"I appreciated that he was the kind of manager who allowed you to play. Red was responsible for me winning so many games. He would leave me in there in the seventh, eighth, ninth innings when a lot of times I probably should have been taken out."

— **Bob Gibson, the winningest pitcher in Cardinals history, on Red Schoendienst, the winningest Cardinals manager**

Cardinals manager Red Schoendienst debates umpire Frank Umont as Boston skipper Dick Williams listens.

RIGHT: "El Birdos" celebrate their 5-2 victory in Game 3 of the 1967 World Series. From left are catcher Tim McCarver, pitcher Nelson Briles, first baseman Orlando Cepeda and second baseman Julian Javier. "El Birdos" was the nickname pinned on the '67 Cardinals by coach Joe Schultz.

Cards' king of the hill

Summer 1968

"When bleacher tickets for the '68 World Series went on sale, four of us talked our parents into letting us camp out overnight on the sidewalk outside Busch Stadium to buy tickets. ... One of us managed to grab a couple pints of blackberry brandy from his parents' liquor cabinet, and we made a night of it.

"In the morning, bunnies from the Playboy Club brought everybody coffee and doughnuts, which was a thrill for a bunch of 15-year-old boys. When the line began to move, one of us kicked over an empty brandy bottle, making quite a noise. And wouldn't you know it? Right across from us, waiting in line, stood the pastor of our church."

— R.B. Hayes, Atlanta

In the history of St. Louis sports, no figure has been more fierce or formidable than Bob Gibson. The maturation of "Gibby" as one of baseball's dominant genes coincided with the Cardinals' move into new Busch Stadium. Gibson would have four 20-victory seasons while occupying the mound at Stadium Plaza, and might have had a fifth if he hadn't been felled by a Roberto Clemente line drive in 1967. In a Hall of Fame career that included 251 victories and 3,117 strikeouts, Gibson built his reputation as the game's premier "big game" hunter in the 1960s, pitching seven consecutive complete-game World Series victories at one point. No season defined Gibson's career more distinctly than 1968, which remains among the most remarkable pitching performances in history. "Hoot" won 22 games, and five of his 13 shutouts came consecutively. Thirty-seven years later, his 1.12 earned-run average remains the single-season standard in the National League record book. "Rapid Robert" won both the Cy Young and the MVP awards in the National League, and he continued his mastery as the Cardinals met the Detroit Tigers in the Fall Classic. On Oct. 2 at Busch Stadium, Gibson struck out a World Series-record 17 batters, outdueling 31-game winner Denny McLain and shutting out the Tigers 4-0. But, ironically, Gibson's most dynamic season ended with his biggest disappointment. With the Cardinals and Tigers knotted at three games apiece, Gibson started Game 7 in front of 54,692 at Busch Stadium. He blanked the Tigers for six innings, but center fielder Curt Flood's slip in the seventh inning opened a can of runs for the Tigers. Potbellied Mickey Lolich and his Motor City mates upset the mighty Gibson. ∎

Some fans go to extraordinary lengths to see a 1968 World Series game. Robert Reed is perched atop a trash can in a standing-room area at Busch Stadium.

RIGHT: Cardinals catcher Tim McCarver congratulates Bob Gibson after his 17-strikeout performance in a 4-0 victory in Game 1.

MOMENTS

Gibson has become incomparable, St. Louis' Superman in baseball flannels. He is such an intense competitor that he doesn't like it if his 11-year-old daughter beats him at tic-tac-toe.

— Hall of Fame sportswriter Bob Broeg, writing for the Post-Dispatch in 1968

Bob Gibson takes batting practice at the 1968 World Series. The Hall of Famer was a threat at the plate over a 17-year career, hitting 24 regular-season home runs and two in World Series games.

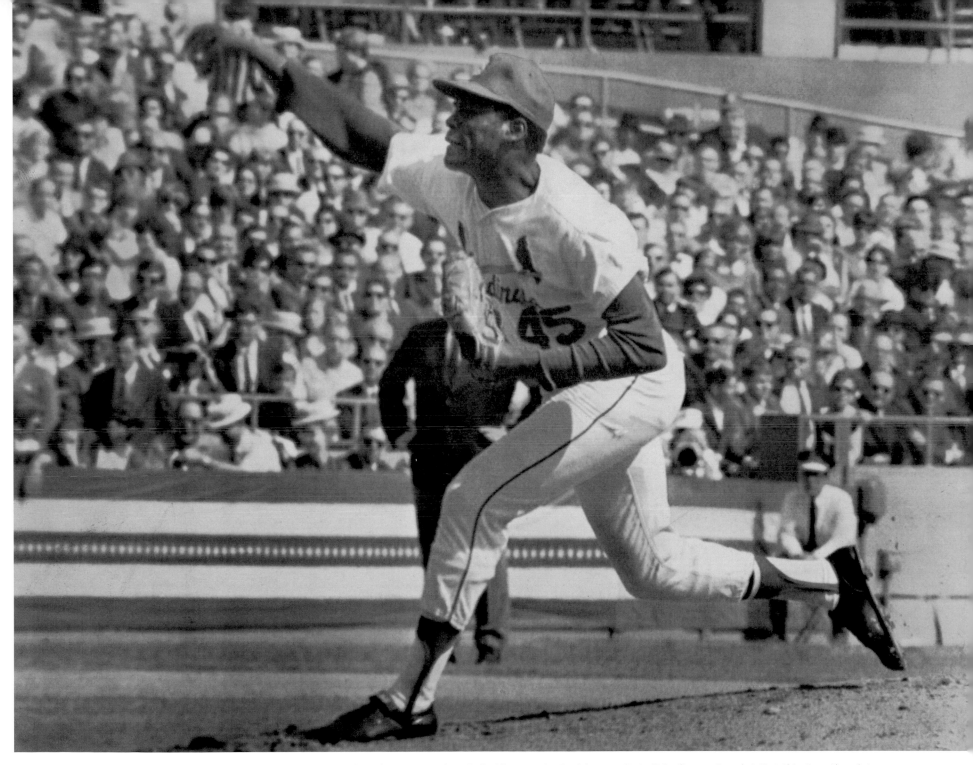

In Game 7 at Busch Stadium, the Cardinals give the ball to their star pitcher, Bob Gibson, who had beaten Detroit in Games 1 and 4. But this time the victory, and the championship, go to the Tigers, 4-1. For Gibson, it's a disappointing end to one of the most brilliant seasons for a pitcher in baseball history.

MOMENTS

"My dad had never gone to a baseball game in his life, let alone a Cardinal game, when his boss offered him two tickets to the first game of the '68 World Series. I was at boot camp in San Diego, soon to ship out to Vietnam.

"I hatched a scheme to get a 72-hour pass to 'participate in a wedding.' Somehow I got the pass, bought a round-trip ticket to St. Louis, my dad picked me up at Lambert and we got to Busch in time to see Gibby make the first pitch.

"I was several hours late on the return to San Diego, but this time I told the truth and shared the story about my dad. The guard had just returned from Vietnam, so he gave me a break, and logged in that I got there just before my pass expired.

"I will never forget that day. It was the only game we ever attended together."

— **Charles Ward, Newberry, S.C.**

In the upper reaches of Busch Stadium, fans rise to applaud Cardinals pitcher Bob Gibson after he sets a World Series record with his 17th strikeout.

RIGHT: Disappointed Cardinals fans leave Busch Stadium after St. Louis' loss to Detroit in Game 7. "It's hard to put into words your feelings when you have just lost the seventh game of the World Series, something I have never experienced before," Cardinals starter Bob Gibson said. "I feel terrible. That's the strongest word I can think of at the moment."

Big Red roost

1966

Baseball wasn't the only big-league sport to call Busch Memorial Stadium home. After 40 years in Chicago, the NFL Cardinals moved to St. Louis in 1960 and transferred into the new downtown facility for the 1966 season. With its movable seating sections, the symmetrical stadium was built to accommodate the birds of a different leather. The football Cardinals made their regular-season debut on the new field with a dramatic 16-13 victory over the Philadelphia Eagles on Sept. 11, 1966, as Jim Bakken's 27-yard field goal with five seconds remaining spelled the difference. But the first season at Busch Stadium would depreciate into the type of disappointment that characterized many of the Big Red's 28 seasons in St. Louis. Torpedoed by injuries, the team saw its fast start become a slow fade and St. Louis would finish fourth in the Eastern Conference. The rest of the decade was similarly volatile, both on and off the field. Emblematic of the times, racial issues came to the forefront after the 1967 season. A contingent of black players presented coach Charley Winner with a list of grievances, one of which called for an assistant coach to be fired. The uneasiness subsided as the team finished strong in 1968, but in an era when the NFL playoffs were harder to crack, its 9-4-1 record was good enough for only second place. Two-time All-Pro offensive tackle Ernie McMillan, who toiled from 1961 to 1974 for the Cardinals, once summed up the experience thusly: "If there is one word to describe playing with the Cardinals, it would have to be 'frustration.' We came so close so often. We had some good teams, had some great teams, but we never seemed to be able to put it all together." ∎

Stadium crew members fasten the base of a goal post in preparation for the first football game at Busch Stadium, an exhibition between the Cardinals and Atlanta on Aug. 6, 1966.

Busch Stadium's movable grandstands are repositioned to accommodate football for the Aug. 6, 1966, exhibition game. Although the circular stadium seems ill-suited for a rectangular sport, Post-Dispatch sports editor Bob Broeg reports that the Big Red's new home was "as delightful for football as for baseball."

MOMENTS

"He used to take me to practice every Saturday at Busch Stadium, and me and Larry Wilson's kid and all the others would play catch and run wild on the field. I liked the excitement of it all, but I also liked the way my dad was respected by the community. I can remember wanting to be respected like that."

— Former NFL player Conrad Goode, on growing up in St. Louis with his stepfather, Big Red lineman Irv Goode

A 9-4-1 season for the football Cardinals in 1968 included a 28-28 tie with the Pittsburgh Steelers at Busch Stadium. Here, defensive back Marv Woodson intercepts a pass intended for the Cardinals' Dave Williams.

RIGHT: With an outdoor facility such as Busch Stadium, sitting in the cold for football games was part of the bargain. A crowd of 39,746 turns out in 20-degree weather on Dec. 14, 1968, and sees the Cardinals defeat the Cleveland Browns 27-16.

Showtime for Pele

June 30, 1968

His full name was Edson Arantes do Nascimento. He was expelled from the fourth grade for skipping classes to play "football." He was discovered at age 11 by a former Brazilian soccer star, who brought the young phenom to the skeptical directors of the Santos professional club and said, "This boy will be the greatest football player in the world." He became known as Pele, the "Black Pearl," or, as his mentor predicted, "the greatest player in the world."

And one summer afternoon in 1968, he put his talents on display at Busch Stadium. At the time, he was 27 and the highest-paid athlete on the planet, earning a salary of $341,000 per year. Pele's arrival in St. Louis was part of a national soccer renaissance. After surprisingly high TV ratings for the 1966 World Cup, the North American Soccer League was formed in 1967, with the St. Louis Stars among its charter members. The Stars played their home games in the new downtown stadium, featuring local standouts such as Pat McBride and foreign imports such as

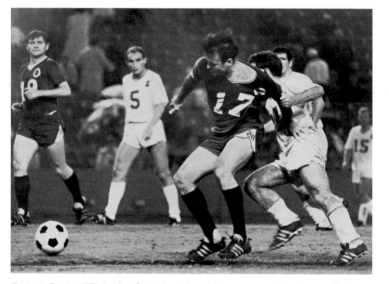

Pat McBride (17) is the first American-born player to sign and play in the North American Soccer League. He played at Busch Stadium for the St. Louis Stars from 1967-76.

Casey Frankiewicz. On Sunday, June 30, 1968, with the mercury rising to 95 degrees in St. Louis, 20,116 watched the Stars play exhibition host to Santos of Brazil. And the star of the show did not disappoint. Pele gathered in a long pass with 28 minutes remaining and flipped a shot over Stars goalie Barney Vidinic for the game-winning tally in Santos' 3-2 victory. Pele would return to Busch Stadium in 1977 as a member of the New York Cosmos. ■

MOMENTS

"We're not accustomed to the sun. It is hot in Brazil, but we play our games in the evening."

— Pele, after playing a Sunday afternoon game at Busch in 95-degree heat

Mike Kalicanin (left) of the Stars does everything he can to stop the great Pele. But in the end, Pele gets the winning goal because, as St. Louis manager Rudi Gutendorf said, "Pele is the god of soccer and the referee let him play like one."

'Meet me at the statue'

Aug. 4, 1968

"Growing up in Lawrence-ville, Ill., a trip to St. Louis was like going to the Land of Oz. The Arch. The city skyline. And especially Busch Stadium, home of my Cardinals.

"My first trip was like a religious experience. It was the day they dedicated Stan Musial's statue. I had only heard of the greatness of Stan the Man, and to see him in uniform that day — if only to jog out and wave to the fans — was unforgettable."

— Cardinals fan
John Sauerhage

Stan Musial was never a fixture inside Busch Memorial Stadium, ending his illustrious playing career after 1963, three years before the new downtown stadium opened. But "MUSIAL" became a vibrant figure just outside the gates, where fans and friends gathered, where a city's skyline and its proud baseball tradition merged into a single bronze form. The Musial statue at the stadium's entrance at Broadway and Walnut Street was commissioned by the Baseball Writers Association of America, sculpted by Carl Mose and dedicated on Sunday, Aug. 4, 1968. In conjunction with the statue unveiling, Musial and members of the 1941 Cardinals — the team he broke in with — took the field before the Cardinals-Cubs game that afternoon. While the other former Cardinals took their positions in street clothes, Stan "The Man" received a deafening ovation from the crowd of 47,445 when he dashed to his outfield position wearing his familiar No. 6 uniform. At the statue dedication afterward, Musial's mother, Mary, and his wife, Lil, pulled the string to unveil the sculpture in the area that expanded to include the "Plaza of Champions" in 1995. "Today, I feel like I'm 18 feet tall," Musial said during his speech, and he was close to being correct. The bronze figure in batting pose actually is 10 feet 5 inches tall and stands on a marble pedestal that is $8\frac{1}{2}$ feet tall. Inscribed on the statue are the words Commissioner Ford Frick used to describe Musial upon his retirement: "HERE STANDS BASEBALL'S PERFECT WARRIOR, HERE STANDS BASEBALL'S PERFECT KNIGHT." ■

Stan Musial's mother, Mary, kisses The Man of the hour after helping dedicate his statue.

MOMENTS

"I want to thank everyone — for my mother and the Musial family — for making me a Cardinal forever."

— Stan Musial, upon the unveiling of his statue

Stan Musial addresses a crowd that includes his wife, Lil, and his mother, Mary.

MOMENTS

In analyzing an event like Superjam, it can be hard to separate the quality of the music from the sociology of the event. In other words, when the music is less than satisfactory, one can always point out that the members of the crowd have one another — all 45,000 of them — and a lovely day at Busch Stadium.

— Post-Dispatch story on Superjam, a midsummer celebration of rock music in the late 1970s

The
1970s

BY DAN O'NEILL OF THE POST-DISPATCH

W hen it opened in 1966, Busch Memorial Stadium was trumpeted as a multipurpose facility. During the 1970s, the proof was in the pliability. Built to be baseball-football ambidextrous, the ballpark became even more adaptable in 1970 when synthetic turf was installed. Because the field was below street level, with portions of the stadium receiving only limited amounts of sun and air flow, growing and maintaining grass in the enclosure had become problematic. The AstroTurf not only provided a consistent surface, it virtually eliminated rain checks and made it possible to convert the facility from baseball to football or special events in a matter of hours. During the decade, the stadium made the most of its versatility. The annual Bronze Boot soccer game between St. Louis University and Southern Illinois University Edwardsville drew crowds in excess of 20,000 at its peak. And in 1977, the largest crowd at a pro soccer game in St. Louis history— 32,605 — saw the Stars defeat international superstar Pele and the New York Cosmos 2-0.

Late on a Saturday afternoon in July 1977, fans wait for the start of Superjam '77, which features REO Speedwagon, Ted Nugent, Head East, Gypsy and Judas Priest. The crowd exceeds 45,000 and the temperature reaches 92 degrees — a bit too warm for Judas Priest guitarist Glenn Tipton. "It was burning the toes of my boots today," he said.

THE 1970s

The stadium also welcomed high school football. Archrivals St. Louis U. High and CBC played annually in the big house, and in 1979, Missouri's high school athletic association debuted its Show-Me Bowl football championships at Busch.

Ten years after the stadium played host to the Beatles concert, rock 'n' roll returned with Superjam '76, the first in a series of the mega-rock concerts at the ballpark. More than 40,000 gathered for the initial blast, which featured a variety of groups, a variety of controlled substances and lots of trash to pick up afterward.

In addition to music, there was mirth. Events such as the Moolah Shrine Circus became annual summertime attractions. And there were missionaries, as the Jehovah's Witnesses twice staged inspirational rallies at Busch before as many as 40,000 people.

Cardinals baseball continued to be the primary stadium tenant. The club came frustratingly close to division titles in 1973 and 1974, finishing 1 1/2 games back each time, but it could not match its rousing success of the 1960s and went the entire decade without a postseason appearance.

"We had a number of characters," said catcher Ted Simmons, a mainstay of the '70s teams. "We didn't have enough ballplayers."

While baseball was still the principal occupant of the stadium, it was not necessarily the top attraction. Attendance sagged during the decade. The team averaged slightly more than 1.5 million at the gate from 1970 to 1979, dipping below that figure three times.

The 1970s marks the end of one era and the beginning of another. Hall of Fame safety Larry Wilson (above) plays his last game in 1972, two years before the beginning of the reign of the Cardiac Cardinals.

ST. LOUIS MOMENTS

1970
More than 2,000 protesters set fire to the Air Force ROTC building at Washington University as they chant "Kent State, Kent State" and "Let it burn!"

1971
Despite City Hall's effort to pass an anti-obscenity ordinance, the musical "Hair" — which includes 20 seconds of nudity — opens at the American Theater downtown.

1972
Minnie Liddell and the Concerned Parents of North St. Louis raise money with raffles, dances and barbecues to file the lawsuit that will lead to the area's school desegregation plan.

1973
An Ozark Air Lines jet crashes near Florissant Road and Interstate 70, killing 38 in St. Louis' worst air disaster.

1974
More nudes than usual on display at the Art Museum as a new national pastime — streaking — finds its way to the museum and other places in the city.

A December snowfall helps to put a colorfully lit Busch Stadium in the holiday spirit in 1979.

1975
Laclede's Landing Redevelopment Corp. is formed to convert a nine-block area north of downtown from a dreary warehouse district to a nightlife center.

1976
Brothers Leon and Michael Spinks, who grew up in the Darst-Webbe housing complex in St. Louis, win boxing gold medals at the Montreal Olympics.

1977
Brewing of Falstaff beer in St. Louis ends after a 127-year run, leaving Anheuser-Busch as the only operating brewery in a city that once had as many as 50.

1978
Strike shuts down both St. Louis daily newspapers, the Post-Dispatch and the Globe-Democrat, for 53 days.

1979
Officials tie a yellow ribbon around the McDonnell Planetarium, a symbol of remembrance and solidarity with Iranian hostage Rocky Sickmann of nearby Krakow, Mo.

Third baseman Ken Reitz (left), catcher Ted Simmons and first baseman Keith Hernandez rush to congratulate Bob Forsch after Forsch pitches a no-hitter against Philadelphia on April 16, 1978 — the first no-hitter at Busch Stadium. A crowd of only 11,495 is there, but its enthusiasm gives Forsch a lift. "With all that cheering when I went out in the ninth, I felt I could lick the world," he said.

"A lot of it had to do with the football Cardinals doing so well," pitcher Bob Forsch recalled. "All summer, people were just waiting for football season — which was good for us. The Cardinals tradition took a hike in the '70s. We were playing bad baseball, and people weren't going to pay for it. We were a pretty boring team at the end of the '70s."

As excitement for the Cardinals waned, a city raised on baseball became infatuated with football. Since moving from Chicago to St. Louis in 1960, the football Cardinals had been a frustrating enigma. Often talented, often injury-jinxed and always inconsistent, the team was a roller-coaster tease of rising expectations and deflating hopes. But when owner Bill Bidwill hired little-known head coach Don Coryell in 1973, the landscape changed. Quietly intense, fiercely competitive, Coryell pumped life into a frumpy franchise with entertaining offenses and heart-stopping finishes. The team known as the Big Red became better known as the Cardiac Cardinals, the NFL's most exhilarating thrill ride.

After consecutive 4-9-1 seasons from 1971 to 1973, Coryell karma took hold in 1974. The Cardinals raced to a stunning 7-0 start on their way to winning their first division championship in St. Louis. They clinched the NFC East with a come-from-behind victory over the New York Giants on the last day of the season, Dec. 15, 1974, celebrating in front of a roaring crowd at Busch Stadium.

Bidwell's bunch won the division again in 1975, posting a record of 11-3, and eight Cardinals were named to the Pro Bowl, including quarterback Jim Hart, electrifying scatback Terry Metcalf and future Hall of Fame tackle Dan Dierdorf. A 10-4 season followed, but then the music stopped.

After a mediocre 7-7 finish in 1977, Coryell departed to San Diego, Metcalf signed to play in Canada and the Cardiac kicks were over. The Cardinals finished out the decade with consecutive losing seasons. Crisp Sunday afternoons at Busch Stadium would never be quite as vibrant. ∎

The ultimate catch of Jackie Smith's Hall of Fame career takes place against Dallas in 1974, when he breaks five tackles and bulls into the Busch Stadium end zone with three Cowboys riding him. Coach Don Coryell calls it "a superhuman effort," and the Cardiac Cardinals pull out a 31-28 victory.

Grass goes artificial

April 1970

Depending on your point of view, it was the worst of surfaces or the best of surfaces. After the 1969 baseball season, Civic Center Redevelopment Corp. elected to follow the crowd and install artificial grass at Busch Stadium. Factors such as climate, soil and drainage combined to make maintaining a natural grass field difficult. The fact was clearly demonstrated by the patchy, thin playing fields that characterized the initial summers downtown. AstroTurf first captured national attention in Houston, where it made baseball possible inside the enclosed Astrodome. Soon ballparks across the land were making the switch to the durable, versatile synthetic. The conversion made sense for multipurpose Busch Stadium. More than 25 percent of the Cardinals' audience was regional, meaning out-of-town fans planned vacations and made sojourns to St. Louis based on seeing baseball. The water-proof pad made rain checks a thing of the past. The AstroTurf floor also allowed the facility to hold other events with a minimal turnover time. The field surface could convert from baseball or football to circus big top in just a few hours. Still, there were drawbacks. The grass-stained uniforms that were once emblematic of Cardinals teams such as the Gashouse Gang became obsolete. "Those hustle marks and stains were something you'd identify with all-out tenacity," Lou Brock said in 1978. "Now you rarely see a player dive for a ball — that stuff can burn you really bad." AstroTurf was figuratively hot at the time, but it was literally hot as well. Midway through the surface's inaugural 1970 season, a study showed the AstroTurf reached 120 degrees four feet from the surface on a sunny, 81-degree day. The new surface debuted on April 10, 1970, as 45,960 watched the Cardinals beat the Mets 7-3. ∎

Brooms replace lawnmowers at the stadium after the grass field gives way to "the rug" for the 1970 baseball season.

Workers lay the first AstroTurf surface at Busch Stadium in March 1970. Several months earlier, James P. Hickok, president of Civic Center, had endorsed AstroTurf with a comment that would fail to pass the test of time: "Recent surveys have shown a marked reduction in the incidence of knee and ankle injuries to athletes who practice and play on the Monsanto surface."

Heart-stopping football

1974-76

MOMENTS

"Back in 1975, the Big Red's mortal enemies were the Cowboys and Redskins. I had no love for 'America's Team,' but I hated the Redskins with a passion.

"So that famous Mel Gray TD reception was sweeter than good — because I don't think Gray held on long enough for a TD. It was before instant replay, so there wasn't the scrutiny there is today. Once the zebras declared it a catch, it was a done deal.

"The Washington fans went nuts, calling it a 'phantom catch.' There were calls for an investigation. It was wild! And, of course, the perfect salve for long-suffering St. Louis fans."

— Big Red fan Curt Parker, recalling the 1975 game at Busch Stadium

For most of their 28 seasons in St. Louis, the football Cardinals were a team that often had talent but rarely had success, a team that seemed to follow each leap forward with a hasty retreat. Then again, there were those three fabulous years. ... From 1974 to 1976, the Big Red morphed into the Cardiac Cardinals, a team that reflected its charismatic coach, Don Coryell, a team that pumped new life into a football-famished town. Those Cardinals won 31 of 42 games and two division titles. But it was more than that. It was the manner in which they played, with Jim Hart's powerful arm, with Terry Metcalf's breathtaking elusiveness, with Dan Dierdorf's grit and determination, with Roger Wehrli's confidence and class. It was the manner in which they won, straddling the fine line between desperation and exhilaration. Twenty-four of the 42 games were decided by a touchdown or less. And perhaps no game epitomized what the "Cardiac" experience was all about more than a 20-17 victory over Washington at Busch Stadium on Nov. 16, 1975. The Cardinals

Cardinals players point to an official who signaled a touchdown after Mel Gray's catch on one of the most controversial plays in the team's 28 seasons in St. Louis.

trailed 17-10 when a final drive took them to the 6-yard line. With 25 seconds remaining, with no timeouts left, Hart dropped back and offered one last prayer. His pass found Mel Gray in the end zone — Gray clutched the ball momentarily before Pat Fischer dislodged it with a ferocious hit. One official immediately signaled touchdown. Another signaled incomplete. With a stadium full of fans stuck in frozen animation, the officials huddled. Finally, the zebras spoke in one voice — "Touchdown!" Jim Bakken kicked a game-winning field goal in sudden-death overtime to send the Cardinals on their way to a division title. Just another day at the office for the Cardiac Cards. ■

Cardinals coach Don Coryell gives instructions to a huddle that includes Conrad Dobler (left), Earl Thomas (82) and Jim Otis (35) before overtime of the game against the Washington Redskins in 1975. The Big Red live up to their Cardiac Cardinals reputation with a 20-17 victory.

MOMENTS

"We gave St. Louis — not just St. Louis, the NFL — some exciting times. We were the original Cardiac Cardinals! We had Jim Hart. We had Mel Gray. We had myself. We had Conrad Dobler. We had Dan Dierdorf. We had some stars. There's a lot of memories there. A lot of good memories."

— Big Red running back Terry Metcalf

The Cardiac Cardinals' most dazzling player is halfback Terry Metcalf, who tries to outrun New York Giants safety Brad Van Pelt in a 1975 game at Busch Stadium.

RIGHT: A fan runs onto the field and "gives some skin" to Cardinals wide receiver Ike Harris after a 31-17 victory over the Dallas Cowboys in 1975.

MOMENTS

"At a cold December game (in 1972), I had on every pair of socks that I owned, several pairs of gloves, earmuffs, hats, and I was still miserable. The Cardinals were on their own 1-yard line, so I decided to go to the only place in the stadium with heat: the restroom.

"No sooner was I in there than a huge roar came from the stands. I fought my way back out to my seat and found out the Cardinals were on the OTHER team's 1-yard line! Jim Hart had completed a 98-yard pass (to Bobby Moore) — the longest non-scoring pass in the history of the NFL. And I was in the john."

— Big Red fan Kurt Ahle, Tokyo

Tough enough to last 18 seasons with the Big Red, quarterback Jim Hart absorbs a hit from Dallas' Harvey Martin.

Former Cardinals tight end Jackie Smith consoles an ex-teammate, Big Red quarterback Jim Hart, after Smith and the Dallas Cowboys win 24-21 in overtime at Busch Stadium in 1978.

MOMENTS

"Game 1 of 1979 brought new life to the football Cardinals franchise, especially in the eyes of a 12-year-old watching from the upper deck. Ottis Anderson makes his NFL debut and runs wild against the Cowboys, racking up a single-game rushing record. But the Cowboys prevail again when a last-second Cardinal field goal falls short. Renewed hope for the franchise? Nah, the Cardinals went on to their usual 5-11 record."

— **Big Red fan Chris Murphy**

The Big Red Line welcomes the team onto the field for a game against the Steelers in 1979, a year that offers little to cheer about.

Brock rocks Busch

Sept. 10, 1974

Philadelphia's Dick Ruthven was on the mound; Cardinals infielder Ron Hunt was at the plate. It was the seventh inning of a lopsided game, an otherwise stagnant September evening at Busch Stadium. And yet, if you were there, it was electric. In what would become one of the defining moments of his illustrious career, Lou Brock broke from first base on an 0-1 pitch, accelerating with each step, defying the miles all those years had put on those 35-year-old legs. A crowd of more than 30,000 at Busch Stadium rose to its feet simultaneously, lifted by the spirit of anticipation. Catcher Bob Boone's throw was late, and Brock slid into second undeterred, the 105th stolen base of his season. As Brock dusted himself off, he dusted off Maury Wills' single-season major league record of 104 steals, and the stadium exploded with adulation. Brock would expand the mark to 118 before the schedule was done, but that captivating moment on Sept. 10, 1974, would become as treasured as any the stadium would know. Cardinals rushed from the dugout to mob the new Prince of Thieves. While there

Lou Brock beats the throw to Philadelphia shortstop Larry Bowa and sets a major league record with his 105th stolen base on Sept. 10, 1974.

were many distinguished players and spectacular capsules to recall from the 1970s, the dynamic Brock was the constant. The Cardinals went the entire decade without a division title, but Brock kept things hopping. He batted over .300 and stole more than 50 bases seven times during the period. As he turned 39, Brock finished the 1978 season with an embarrassing .221 batting average. Most suggested the game and relentless time had finally caught up with "The Base Burglar." But the proud No. 20 came back for one more remarkable season, batting .304 and stealing 21 bases at age 40. Before he was done, he also gave Busch Stadium one last keepsake. On Aug. 13, 1979, Brock slammed a pitch off the leg of Cubs pitcher Dennis Lamp for the 3,000th hit of his career, effectively clearing wall space for a plaque at Cooperstown. ∎

MOMENTS

The spectators jumped to their feet, shouting and clapping in a tumultuous roar. Confetti flew like snow in the left-field bleachers. Celebrants threw wadded paper cups and streamers of toilet paper onto the field. Firecrackers popped. Most people screamed their adoration, and a few wept.

— Post-Dispatch story on stolen base No. 105 for Lou Brock

Hall of Famer James "Cool Papa" Bell joins in the celebration as Lou Brock addresses the crowd after his 105th stolen base. Bell, a superb base thief during his career in the old Negro Leagues, presents Brock with second base. "They decided to give him this base so he could take it home," Bell said. "If not, he'd steal it anyway."

MOMENTS

"To be respectable became
critical to me during the
1970s. Some of the years,
there really wasn't much
for our fans to get excited
about. We weren't always
winning much. For really
quality performances,
sometimes I was it, and
I knew I had to be it."

— **Hall of Famer Lou Brock**

Lou Brock and Cardinals owner August A. Busch Jr. wear Brockabrellas on a hot August day at the stadium in 1976.
Brockabrellas were a reflection of the businessman in Brock — he marketed them through a company that he owned.

A peek into the Cardinals clubhouse before a 1979 game reveals that some players light up, others limber up, as demonstrated by, from left, Keith Hernandez, Pete Vuckovich and Lou Brock.

MOMENTS

"I got my 1,000th hit the night Lou got his 3,000th, and I got one telegram. It said, 'Congratulations on your accomplishment. Wishing you much more success. (Signed) The Lou Brock family.'

"When a man gets his 3,000th hit that night and he still has time to send me a telegram ... that's going into my scrapbook as a prized possession, more than my Gold Glove or anything else. It gave me goose bumps to get something like that from Lou."

— **Cards third baseman Ken Reitz**

Lou Brock spends a moment in the Cardinals dugout with one of his biggest fans — his daughter Wanda.

RIGHT: Lou Brock takes a spin around the field in the 33-foot cabin cruiser given to him by the Cardinals on "Lou Brock Day," Sept. 9, 1979.

The lost decade

MOMENTS

"I remember one year, Mr. Busch, who very rarely came around the ballpark in those days, came into the clubhouse. We were fighting with the Mets for last place, and he told us, 'Whatever you do, finish in front of the Mets.'

"That's when reality slapped us in the face. You know you're going bad when your owner has to ask you not to finish last."

— Cards pitcher Bob Forsch, recalling baseball at Busch in the 1970s

A fter the final game of a frustrating season in 1969, manager Red Schoendienst found a bottle of champagne waiting for him in his Busch Stadium office. The attached card from two Redbirds fans read: "Here's to a first-place champagne party next year." The Redhead said: "I'm storing the bottle right now." But he never got to break out the bubbly during the 1970s, a lost decade for the Cardinals. Schoendienst was fired after a dismal 1976 season, followed by the firings of managers Vern Rapp and Ken Boyer by the time the 1980s rolled around. The Cardinals were in only two pennant races in the '70s, both of which ended in last-day disappointment. Still, there were fulfilling moments and compelling figures. Slugger Dick Allen wowed St. Louis fans with 34 home runs in just 122 games in 1970, the first Cardinal to crack the 30-homer mark since the club moved into its cavernous new environs. Joe Torre kept crowds buzzing the next season by batting a National League-best .363 and winning a National League MVP award, and in 1978, Bob Forsch pitched the first of his two no-hitters at Busch. Bob Gibson and Lou Brock played out the remainder of their careers in the decade. On July 17, 1974, at Busch Stadium, "Gibby" fanned Reds outfielder Cesar Geronimo to become the second pitcher in major league history to strike out 3,000 batters. Brock punched his Cooperstown ticket with several spectacular seasons in the '70s, as chants of "Lou, Lou, Lou" became a summer ritual. Ted Simmons anchored the Cardinals lineup with 1,550 hits — more than any other catcher in baseball in the '70s. And Keith Hernandez matched Torre by winning the batting title and sharing the MVP award in '79. "But it wasn't enough," Simmons said. "Whatever we had, it wasn't nearly enough." ∎

Ken Boyer tries to steer the Cardinals out of their 1970s doldrums, but his three-year run as manager ends in 1980 with a record of 166-190.

Joe Torre often carried the Cardinals on his back in the early '70s, but he gives Atlanta shortstop Felix Millan some support on this play in a 1970 game.

Rock fans jam stadium

1976-78

MOMENTS

When the gates opened three hours early, it was a spectacle, something like the citizens of Rome welcoming the conquering American Army. The young persons ran onto the field cheering, waving and holding their arms over their heads like conquering heroes.

Within a few hours, some of them felt conquered instead. The first-aid station at the stadium reported 200 cases of heat exhaustion and alcohol and drug abuse. Four youths were taken to City Hospital for alcohol and drug abuse. All were unconscious.

— **Post-Dispatch story on Superjam '77**

When architects designed Busch Stadium, they likely never envisioned their House of Cards might become a House of Rock. But on June 29, 1976, the concrete sports coliseum turned into a guitar-screaming sound garden. "Superjam '76" became the first rock show at the ballpark, the first major concert since the Beatles played Busch on a wet, chilly night 10 years earlier. More than 40,000 attended the multiband extravaganza, toting coolers, toking joints and soaking up Jefferson Starship and Ted Nugent tunes that began at 5 p.m. and echoed off downtown buildings until well after midnight. Some 200 people needed treatment at the five first-aid stations set up in the stadium. While "perhaps a dozen" of those were diagnosed to be suffering from drug overdoses, city policemen working the event assumed a "no harm, no foul" stance toward controlled substances. As one policeman explained, it was leniency by necessity: "How are you going to arrest 40,000 people?" In 1977, Superjam drew a crowd of more than 45,000, the largest to see a musical event in St. Louis to that point. Again, the gathering generally was well-behaved, although a mischievous group tried to break into the Stadium Club and shattered its glass doors. Superjams and other music festivals continued to be staged at the stadium throughout the decade and into the early 1980s, as bands such as REO Speedwagon, Blue Oyster Cult, Styx, Judas Priest and Head East brought high decibels and high energy to the stage. "All I remember is that it was hot on the AstroTurf and it was a lot of people," recalled St. Louisan Michael Levinson, who was 23 when he attended Superjam in 1978. "And it was the place to be." ■

Fans at Superjam '78 stand atop their coolers for a better view.

RIGHT: A 1977 crowd of 45,000 withstands heat that is recorded at 92 degrees at 3 p.m. Despite "a couple of drug overdoses, mainly it's been problems with standing the heat," said a spokesman for Acid Rescue.

MOMENTS

"I think I attended five or six Superjams — I was at the first one and remember Stevie Nicks in her witchy dress and Uncle Ted in his white jumpsuit with the tail. The concerts were general admission, and the tarps on the field were always incredibly sticky within an hour of the gates opening. They were my first intro-duction to the 'festival' type of concert — a lesson in endurance!"

— **St. Louisan Deborah Doyle**

Fans wait for the start of Superjam '78 after camping outside the stadium through the night.

A spectator's binoculars provide a better view of Superjam '78, which features Styx, Blue Oyster Cult, Angel, Eddie Money and Bob Welch.

MOMENTS

"When the gates opened, there was a massive surge of stoners cramming and shoving everyone trying to get in. I ended up being picked up and carried over the turnstiles by the crowd. I had a pony beer in my hand and it never spilled. The ticket people never saw me go over.

"The Acid Patrol was everywhere making sure no one overdosed. If you sat down, they would run over and ask you what you were on. You would have to take off running so they wouldn't take you in.

"But I will always remember how everybody walked around Busch Stadium talking, dancing, having a great time with no trouble. I didn't see any fights or guns like they worry about nowadays."

— **Carrie L. Lyons, recalling Superjam '76**

Ted Nugent kicks off Superjam '76, belting out what a Post-Dispatch reviewer says is "his standard show of raunchy rock" and "a few blood-curdling screams loud enough to make you wince 400 feet away."

RIGHT: Two of the fans at Superjam '78 make their way off the field through debris left by their fellow spectators.

Drama on a high wire

Summer 1971

MOMENTS

At one point in his high-wire walk over the stadium, Wallenda stopped and placed the balancing pole on the wire and stood on his head. ... As he regained his balance and began walking on the wire again, he wobbled, the balancing pole waving from side to side.
A woman turned to a companion and said: "He's doing that on purpose."

— **Post-Dispatch story on Karl Wallenda's daredevil performance at Busch Stadium**

In 1962, the Flying Wallendas toppled from their "human pyramid" on a circus high wire — a stunt performed without a safety net. Two family members died; another was paralyzed. Another Wallenda died in a fall from the high wire one year later. Would they retire from performing ... or at least start using a safety net? No, these were circus people from Magdeburg, Germany. They loved the performance, they lived the creed: "The show must go on." And in June 1971, the show came to Busch Stadium as part of the Moolah Shrine Circus, which for 25 years turned the downtown ballpark into a carnival big top. To climax the second stadium appearance of the "Circus With a Purpose," a $5/8$-inch metal wire was stretched 600 feet across the roof of the stadium, 160 feet above the hard synthetic surface. And there appeared Karl Wallenda, 66 years of age, holding a 35-foot pole for balance and, as

Lion tamer Paul Anthony has his hands full with one of his animals at the Moolah Shrine Circus at Busch Stadium in 1971.

always, working without a net (he thought it provided a "false sense of security"). If you were among the more than 20,000 in attendance, you couldn't help but hold your breath. Wallenda moved purposefully across the wire, one foot over the other. At one point, he stopped to place the balancing pole on the wire and stand on his head. Several times he paused, the pole wavering from side to side. Twice he stopped to sit down, once to remove a key that had fallen from his sock to the bottom of his shoe. Eleven minutes after he ventured out onto the wire, Wallenda stepped off onto a platform. There would be no fall this time; the crowd roared. "I get a kick out of it," Wallenda said, "but my family thinks I'm crazy." ■

Karl Wallenda, the 66-year-old patriarch of the Flying Wallendas, goes out for an evening stroll — along a wire strung 600 feet across Busch Stadium, 160 feet off the ground, with no safety net. Wallenda's 11-minute walk is the highlight of the Moolah Shrine Circus.

MOMENTS

"I've played big places before, but nothing this size. I bet I'll feel like a midget in there."

— **4-foot-2 Harold Simmons, preparing for his gig as horseback rider, tumbler and clown at the Moolah Shrine Circus in Busch Stadium**

The Shriners' parade passes by the stadium on the night before the circus opens in 1978.

The grounds crew is captivated by the Fearless Bauers of Switzerland as they sway atop 110-foot steel poles at the 1971 circus.

The 1980s

BY DAN O'NEILL OF THE POST-DISPATCH

I f athletes can reach their peak, if ballplayers can reach their prime, then perhaps stadiums do the same. If so, the 1980s might have been Busch Stadium's "career years." No increment in the history of the stadium was more varied or vibrant. No period was more punctuated with compelling moments, unique characters and unshakeable memories. First and foremost, the decade represented a spirited revival of a storied baseball franchise. While individual stars still shined, the once-proud Cardinals had straddled the fence of mediocrity for much of the 1970s, failing to advance to postseason play even once. But in 1980, while the club staggered to a fourth-place finish and drew just 1,385,147 fans, seeds of revival were sewn. That summer, the club fired Ken Boyer as manager and replaced him with Whitey Herzog. The former Kansas City Royals skipper had a way with words and a way with building ballclubs. Herzog ascended to the dual role of general manager later that season and put the franchise back on a pennant-winning path. Structured with speed and defense, custom-fit to their expansive ballpark, the Cardinals won a thrilling seven-game World Series over the Milwaukee Brewers in 1982.

Shortstop Ozzie Smith's acrobatics are just one of the reasons fans flip for the Cardinals in the 1980s.

MOMENTS

"The baseball fans coming back to Busch Stadium — that was the most exciting thing about the 1980s. ... seeing the turnaround from the '70s to the '80s.

"In the '70s, the football Cardinals were the big thing in town. Then, in the 1980s, we drew over 3 million fans in a small market."

— Cardinals pitcher Bob Forsch

"The idea that a community of this size could draw 3 million fans for baseball means that probably man-for-man, pound-for-pound, St. Louis must be one of the finest sports communities in the whole world."

— Baseball commissioner Peter Ueberroth in 1987

Key players in the Cardinals' triumphant summer of 1985 celebrate a sweep of the Mets at Busch. From left are manager Whitey Herzog, shortstop Ozzie Smith, left fielder Vince Coleman, second baseman Tom Herr and pitcher Jeff Lahti.

With 53,723 fans roaring on each pitch, Bruce Sutter struck out Gorman Thomas to seal a 6-3 victory in Game 7, providing the Cardinals their first Series championship in 15 years and Busch Stadium its first home clincher.

"Whiteyball" became part of the vernacular, and St. Louis sprouted its baseball roots like never before. The club averaged attendance of more than 2.5 million from 1982 through 1989 and topped the 3 million mark in 1987 and 1989, two more pennant-race seasons.

Herzog continued to carve his Cardinals legacy by guiding the club to pennants in 1985 and 1987. The Cardinals won 101 games to outlast the "Pond Scum" New York Mets and capture the NL East in '85. The season featured a batting championship (.353) and MVP award for Willie McGee and a Rookie of the Year award for Vince Coleman, who stole 110 bases.

More thrills came in the postseason, when the club rallied from a deficit of two games to none to beat Los Angeles in a dramatic NLCS. Ozzie Smith's walk-off homer in Game 5 allowed 53,708 to "go crazy" on Oct. 14 at Busch Stadium, and Jack Clark's homer in Game 6 wrapped up the pennant. But cheers turned to tears in the "I-70 Series" with neighboring Kansas City. After winning three of the first four games, the Cardinals came apart after umpire Don Denkinger's controversial call in Game 6 and dropped the series in seven games.

ST. LOUIS MOMENTS

1980	**1981**	**1982**	**1983**	**1984**
Midwest heat wave kills 118 in St. Louis, where the temperature hits 100 degrees or higher for 18 days.	The first VP Fair opens on the Arch grounds, and more than 1.5 million people attend what's billed as "America's Biggest Birthday Party."	Late January blizzard shuts down the St. Louis region, with as much as 22 inches of snow measured in some areas. City offers "anyone with a snow plow" $45 an hour to help clear the streets.	EPA announces that the town of Times Beach in far west St. Louis County will be bought out and leveled because of dioxin contamination.	Jackie Joyner-Kersee of East St. Louis begins her historic Olympic career at the Los Angeles Games. She takes home the silver medal in the heptathlon.

Despite mediocre football, the Cardinals draw well in the 1980s. It is only at the very end, in 1987, that attendance dwindles.

1985
Union Station and St. Louis Centre open as retail centers amid elaborate ceremonies and huge traffic jams downtown.

1986
The first Missouri state lottery ticket is sold in January; by the end of the year, almost 275 million "instant" and 10 million "Lotto" tickets are sold, and 11 winners become millionaires.

1987
Five employees of a National supermarket are shot to death as they lie on the floor by gunmen robbing the store on Natural Bridge in St. Louis.

1988
St. Louisan Richard A. Gephardt wins Iowa's Democratic caucuses, a victory that is supposed to launch him on the road to the White House.

1989
The Sun, a tabloid hoping to fill the void created when the Globe-Democrat folded in 1986, begins publishing. It lasts 7 months.

The team followed a similar script in 1987. After another NL East title, the club engaged San Francisco in a contentious NLCS. With Jeffrey "One Flap Down" Leonard pounding home runs, the Giants took a 3-2 lead in the best-of-seven affair. But the final two games of the series were played at Busch Stadium, where the Cardinals found sanctuary. The rallying Redbirds prevailed 1-0 behind John Tudor in a tense Game 6. Bolstered by an unexpected home run by Jose Oquendo and more shutout pitching from Danny Cox and Co., the Cardinals won 6-0 and advanced to their 15th World Series. Again, the Fall Classic proved to be a frustrating finale – Tom Lawless' improbable home run in Game 4

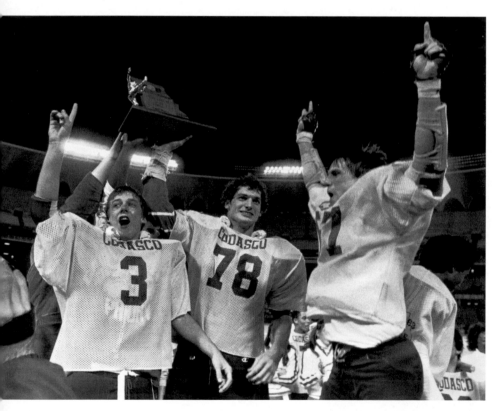

Tom Canfield (3), Steve Tschudy (78) and Dick Disper of Country Day School celebrate a state football title in 1983. Missouri's high school championship games were played at Busch Stadium four times in the 1980s.

notwithstanding. Although the Cardinals won all three games at Busch Stadium and had a 3-2 lead in the series, they lost all four games in the "Homerdome" in Minnesota.

While baseball dominated the landscape in the 1980s, there were many other scrapbook entries, some inspiring, others deflating. Despite exciting players such as Ottis Anderson, Roy Green, Neil Lomax and Stump Mitchell, the football Cardinals never recaptured their success of the mid-1970s. A 9-7 log in 1984 was the team's best of the decade. In the meantime, owner Bill Bidwill publicly complained he could no longer compete financially in the St. Louis environment. Citing oppressive city taxes, calling Busch Stadium too small and antiquated, Bidwill announced he was moving the team to Phoenix after the 1987 season. On Dec. 13, 1987, a modest crowd of 29,623 watched the Cardinals beat the New York Giants 27-24 in their final game at Busch, closing the books on 28 seasons of Big Red football in St. Louis.

Conventional sports represented only part of the busy schedule. The stadium played host to myriad activities, some more extreme than others. The events ranged from the foot-tapping variety (Greater St. Louis Marching Band Festival) to the ear-splitting kind (U.S. Hot Rod Truck Pull & Mud Racing Championships); from distinctly American (Olympic torch run) to international in flavor (Dynamo Minsk of the Soviet Union vs. Team America in exhibition soccer).

The decade at Busch closed with a bang in 1989 when the Who and the Rolling Stones rocked the ballpark in concerts five weeks apart. More than 52,000 came through the gates to see the Stones, including apprentice Mick Jagger fans such as 12-year-old Blake Cunningham and his 11-year-old sister, Jennifer, from Carrollton, Ill. Their parents, Dan and Debbie Cunningham, were happy to spend the $120 to put their foursome in the 12th row. "I wish I'd had the chance to see the Beatles in '66," Dan Cunningham said. "I wanted to make sure my kids got to see the Stones." ■

Roger Daltrey's image appears on a monitor as the Who plays Busch Stadium on Aug. 11, 1989. Noting that members of the band are over 40, the Post-Dispatch predicts that it's probably the Who's last concert in St. Louis and comments, "If that is true, we can say the group went out in style."

Winning with Whiteyball

June 1980

MOMENTS

"I was at Busch Stadium in 1983 the night Whitey traded Keith Hernandez to the Mets. When the announcement was flashed on the scoreboard, a hush fell over the crowd and then a great wave of booing began.

"When Whitey brought out the lineup before the game, I thought the crowd was going to come out of the stands and lynch him. People were so angry they didn't even care that it was one of the rare games in which the Cards beat Steve Carlton.

"It's hard to imagine that so many people now have such fond memories of Whitey; that night, he didn't have a friend anywhere in Busch."

— Cardinals fan Alan Schmidt, Chico, Calif.

The Cardinals endured a decade of disappointing baseball in the 1970s, with nary a pennant to add to their lineage. By 1980, things were bottoming out. Attendance was nose-diving and the club was stumbling along at 18-33 when it decided to fire manager Ken Boyer. And from that darkness came a new dawn, embodied by Dorrel "Whitey" Herzog. Hired to replace Boyer, the New Athens, Ill., native changed the Busch Stadium landscape with bold trades, blunt quotes and refreshing baseball acumen. Hired initially as manager, Herzog soon took over as general manager and tore apart the roster, remaking it with what he called a "winning attitude." During one ferocious five-day period in December 1980, Herzog traded 13 players and acquired eight. The following winter, Herzog was busy again, acquiring future Hall of Fame shortstop Ozzie Smith, among others. By the summer of 1982, the rehab was realizing championship rewards. Herzog guided the Cardinals to a pennant and World Series triumph over the Milwaukee Brewers, the first championship for St. Louis since 1967, the first clinched at Busch Stadium. Herzog credited owner August A. "Gussie" Busch Jr. for giving him the "authority to make the decisions I needed to make." With players such as Lonnie Smith, Ozzie Smith, Vince Coleman, Tom Herr and Willie McGee, Herzog fit his teams to his expansive ballpark, fit them

Cardinals manager Whitey Herzog pulls Garry Templeton off the field on Aug. 26, 1981, after the shortstop makes obscene gestures to the crowd. The next season, Herzog has a new shortstop — Ozzie Smith.

with speed and defense. Playing "Whiteyball," the Cardinals had 200 or more stolen bases for seven consecutive seasons under Herzog. Attendance at Busch soared above the 3 million mark in 1987 and '89. But the match came to an inglorious end in 1990 when Herzog, with his team slumming in last place, abruptly resigned. "I came here in last place," he said, "I leave here in last place." But in between, most Cards fans would be quick to add, it was a heck of a ride. ■

A rainout on Oct. 8, 1982, postpones the NL Championship Series, but brighter days are just around the corner for Whitey Herzog and the Cardinals.

MOMENTS

"Our team was the best team in the 1980s. We had a great manager. We all knew what our roles were. If you didn't run, Whitey was mad. It's a fun-type game. It was always exciting. There was always something going on at a fast pace."

— Cardinals outfielder Willie McGee

The boisterous Cards-Giants rivalry in the 1980s culminates with a bench-clearing scrap at Busch on July 24, 1988. Jose Oquendo and Will Clark trade punches as Ozzie Smith moves in.

RIGHT: In the blink of an eye, it seems, Whitey Herzog turns the Cardinals from losers to winners in the '80s. After three trips to the World Series, Herzog resigns in 1990 when the team hits bottom again.

On top of the world

Oct. 20, 1982

MOMENTS

"A crazy thought came to us on an October afternoon in 1982: How often do we have an opportunity to experience Game 7 of the World Series? We don't have tickets, but it would be fun to hang out around Busch Stadium and soak up the atmosphere.

"We arrived at Busch an hour before the game and saw scalpers selling tickets for $100 apiece. We decided to stand outside by center field — back then, you could see into the stadium. I'll never forget the scene: Gussie Busch was sitting atop the Budweiser wagon pulled by the Clydesdales as they marched around to the tune of 'Here Comes the King.' Then I heard a voice from behind ask if we had tickets.

(continued)

From a baseball fan's standpoint, it is the ultimate experience, a birthday, New Year's Eve and Christmas all rolled into one. And in 1982, for the first time in 18 years, the first time at Busch Stadium, it happened in St. Louis. The Cardinals won a World Series at home. After dismantling the Atlanta Braves in the League Championship Series, the Cardinals met the Milwaukee Brewers in a Fall Classic that was full of subplots. Like St. Louis, Milwaukee was a beer-and-bratwurst type of town, so it was brewery vs. brewery, Budweiser vs. Miller. The American Leaguers featured catcher Ted Simmons and pitcher Pete Vuckovich, former Cardinals of distinction. The Brewers were known as "Harvey's Wallbangers," a reference to manager Harvey Kuenn and a long-ball offense. The Cardinals played "Whiteyball," a reference to manager Whitey Herzog and a speed-and-defense format that managed a grand total of 67 homers. Fittingly, the series see-sawed back and forth, the contrasting styles taking turns dominating. Simmons homered in Game 1 as the Brewers pounded the Cardinals 10-0 at Busch. The Cardinals bounced back to take Game 2, with a walk to Steve Braun forcing home the decisive run. The Brewers lost Game 3 in Milwaukee as Willie McGee blossomed on the national stage, but rallied to win Games 4 and 5 and led the series 3-2 going back to St. Louis. With 25-year-old righthander John Stuper pitching a complete game, weathering nearly three hours of rain delays at Busch Stadium, the Cardinals won 13-1 in Game 6. Joaquin Andujar, who referred to himself as "one tough Dominican," had been knocked out of Game 3 by a Simmons line drive off his right knee. But he showed his mettle by taking the ball — gimpy knee and all — in Game 7. Andujar worked seven innings, and with the help of a three-run rally in the sixth, the Cardinals took a 6-3 lead into the bottom of the ninth. As Busch Stadium's 53,723 fans went wild, closer Bruce Sutter struck out Gorman Thomas and then caught Darrell Porter leaping into his arms as the Cardinals nailed down their ninth world championship. ∎

A couple of buds, Ron Karsten (left) and John Pestal, cheer on the Cardinals at Game 6.

"It was an angel dressed in a suit with an NBC 'peacock' pin on the lapel, and he was holding a handful of tickets. He started counting out four tickets, bul being pragmatic and broke, I said, 'How much?' He said, 'I am giving them to you.'

"We were in total shock as we ran to the gate, and then we looked at the tickets: Section 250, the loge section right behind home plate. It didn't seem real! ... We saw one of the most exciting games ever played at Busch, and in the ninth, we screamed 'Bruuuuuce' on every pitch until I couldn't even talk.

"When the final out came, pandemonium ensued. I had just experienced a dream come true, and to paraphrase Jack Buck, 'That's a miracle!' "

— **Gary L. Vollmer, Wildwood, Mo.**

Rookie Willie McGee's heroics in the 1982 World Series offer a glimpse of what is to come for one of the most popular players in Cardinals history.

MOMENTS

"Most of all, the 1982 team had camaraderie with a capital C. It was a unique group of 25 guys. Everybody just fit on that team.

"Somebody's going to get on somebody's nerves over the course of a season, but everybody kind of let that roll off their backs. I can't recall any friction.

"It was the finest team I've ever played on as far as getting along and cohesion."

— Cardinals first baseman Keith Hernandez

Joaquin "One Tough Dominican" Andujar wins two games in the 1982 World Series, including the decisive seventh at Busch Stadium.

MOMENTS

"Sutter from the belt,
to the plate ...
a swing and a miss!
And that's a winner!
That's a winner!
A World Series winner
for the Cardinals!"

**— Jack Buck,
calling the final out
of Game 7 on KMOX**

Catcher Darrell Porter leaps
into the arms of relief pitcher
Bruce Sutter after Sutter
strikes out the Brewers'
Gorman Thomas for the
final out of Game 7.

MOMENTS

Porter and Sutter barely have time to hug before a sea of people are upon them. The crowd pays no heed to warnings that they would be arrested if they trod upon the field.

Police dogs, mounted police, dozens of ushers can't stem the tide. The fans flow onto the field. The cops get the players off, but the crowd won't leave. Dogs growl and horses prance, but there are too many in this roaring crowd.

Fireworks explode beyond Busch Stadium and still the crowd pours over the walls. They run and dance and rip up strips of AstroTurf. Some fans bend and kiss the turf. It goes on for more than an hour. And you never want it to end.

— **Post-Dispatch archives**

Fans join the celebration on the field after the Cardinals win the franchise's ninth World Series championship.

RIGHT: After a victory in Game 7, champagne flies in the Cardinals clubhouse among celebrants Gene Roof (left), Jeff Lahti (center) and Dave LaPoint.

The land of Ozzie

Oct. 14, 1985

MOMENTS

"Our family was staying at the Marriott across from Busch. I gave Amy, 7, and Adam, 5, a baseball and we went to get autographs. Player after player walked by and everyone said they were too busy to sign.

"It was time to go back to the hotel when the kids shouted, 'There's Ozzie!' All that separated them from Ozzie was a security guard who said, 'Sorry, only players past this door.'

"Ozzie looked at the kids and said, 'Do you want Ozzie's autograph?' The security guard didn't budge, but Ozzie gave him a huge smile and said, 'Sir, let the kids in.' Amy and Adam got an autograph and a conversation with a Hall of Fame shortstop. What a day!"

— **Darrell Davis, Fulton, Mo.**

He was known as "The Wizard of Oz," one Osborne Earl Smith. He created the moniker with an athletic flair that made him one of the most spectacular defensive players in baseball history. He could have an impact on a game with his acrobatic glove the way a slugger could alter it with a monstrous swing. The arrival of Smith in 1982 coincided with the return of championship baseball in St. Louis. And yet his most extraordinary single act, one of the most memorable episodes in the history of Busch Stadium, was the most uncharacteristic moment of his Hall of Fame career. The setting was the National League Championship Series, late on a Monday afternoon in October. The Cardinals had fallen behind the Dodgers by losing the first two games in Los Angeles. But they rallied to win Games 3 and 4 back in St. Louis. With the final two games scheduled for LA, it seemed imperative for the Cardinals to win Game 5 at Busch. Anxiety levels shot upward for the 53,708 spectators as the pivotal game went to the bottom of the ninth, tied 2-2. Dodgers reliever Tom Niedenfuer rocked and fired, hoping to overpower the tiny Smith with a fastball inside. But "The Wizard," all 5 feet 10 and 150 pounds of him, had other ideas. The Wizard had a magic wand. In 3,008 previous major league at-bats lefthanded, Smith had never hit a ball over the fence, but he had never hit a ball like this. The drive soared toward the right-field wall as the crowd's anticipation soared with it. It smacked against one of the concrete pillars, barely above the yellow line, and caromed onto the field. It happened so quickly, so stunningly, no one was certain. But umpire Terry Tata signaled the implausible, broadcaster Jack Buck voiced the unforgettable, and the city of St. Louis erupted in kind. ∎

Unable to perform his traditional backflip on opening day in 1986 because of a shoulder injury, Ozzie Smith has his son O.J., 3, give it a try.

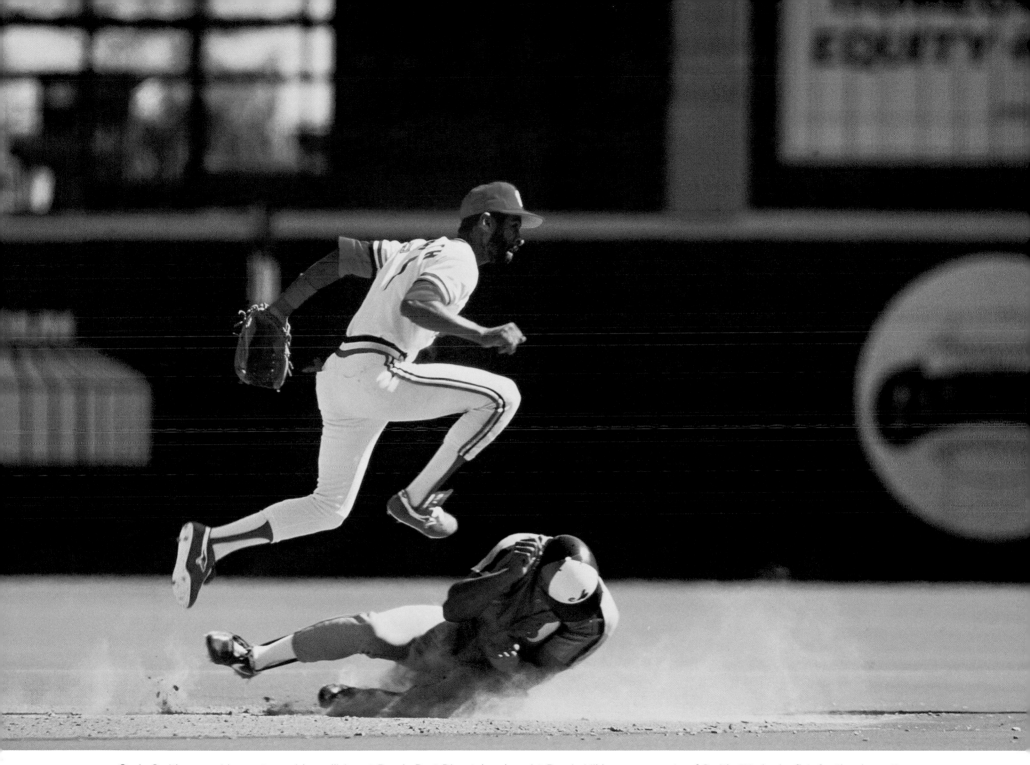

Ozzie Smith goes airborne to avoid a collision at Busch. Post-Dispatch columnist Bernie Miklasz once wrote of Smith: "He had a flair for the dramatic, a hand for magic, a touch of gold. He could make baseballs disappear into his glove. He could fly."

MOMENTS

"Smith corks one into right, down the line. It may go ... Go crazy, folks! Go crazy! It's a home run and the Cardinals have won the game 3-2 on a home run by the Wizard. Go crazy!"

— **Jack Buck,
calling Ozzie's homer
on KMOX**

Ozzie Smith was a wizard with the glove, but his biggest moment as a Cardinal comes when he homers over the right-field wall in the bottom of the ninth to give the Redbirds a 3-2 victory over the Dodgers in Game 5 of the 1985 National League Championship Series.

MOMENTS

"The timing of that was spectacular. It's something a player dreams about. It's something a guy works 162 games for. It's something he'll never forget; it's something we'll never forget.

"All the right buttons were pushed on that one."

— Jack Clark, on Ozzie's "Go Crazy!" homer

The wild and the wacky

Stadium history was made when Mike Laga struck the first ball ever to be hit out of Busch. The only problem was that it was about 150 feet foul. It zoomed over the arch-patterned roof — landing eight stories below.

A Cardinals official said that the distance of the roof from the field was 130 feet and that the ball was found in a flower bed near the employees' parking lot.

Laga was surprised with a standing ovation and then struck out to end the inning. "It was pretty funny," Laga said. "I didn't think about what had happened, until the fans got louder and louder. I thought, 'What's going on here?' I didn't know it was the first one."

— Post-Dispatch coverage of Sept. 15, 1986, Cards game

The history of Busch Stadium includes good moments, bad moments and, if not ugly, certainly unusual moments. Especially in the 1980s. For instance, on April 17, 1983, the term "Whiteyball" took on new meaning when a Cardinals game with the New York Mets — promoted as "Sun Visor Day" — was postponed because of snow. Snow in April was weird, but not nearly as freakish as what happened to outfielder Vince Coleman in the 1985 National League Championship Series. As the Cardinals worked out before Game 4 at Busch, rain began to fall. Coming off the field, Coleman failed to notice the automatic tarp had been engaged to cover the infield. The tarp nabbed the unsuspecting Coleman and rolled over his left leg, leaving the Cardinals without the NL Rookie of the Year for the remainder of the postseason. "Can you imagine a guy who steals all those bases and runs like a rabbit caught in a tarpaulin going 1 mile an hour?" teammate Cesar Cedeño said. Busch's "Seat Cushion Night" on April 18, 1987, was another awkward event. Seat cushions were distributed to fans as they entered the stadium for a game with the "Pond Scum" Mets. When the Cardinals rallied from a 5-0 deficit and took the lead, thousands of fans got over-zealous and sailed their cushions onto the field. The game was halted for six minutes while the stadium crew cleaned up the mess. The Cardinals eventually won 12-8 in extra innings on Tom Herr's grand slam, and another torrent of cushions hit the field. "I guess that will be the end of Seat Cushion Night," manager Whitey Herzog correctly observed. ■

Exuberant fans sail their cushions onto the field after the Cards rally against the Mets on "Seat Cushion Night" in 1987, resulting in extra work for the Busch Stadium grounds crew.

RIGHT: There would be no baseball at the stadium on April 17, 1983, but Cardinals outfielder Lonnie Smith has in mind a little snowball fun.

A farewell to football

Dec. 13, 1987

It began as a rumor in the late 1970s. It graduated to public debate in the mid-1980s and it became reality on March 15, 1988, when NFL owners overwhelmingly approved owner Bill Bidwill's request to move his Cardinals out of St. Louis, to Phoenix. The vote brought an unceremonious end to an unceremonious marriage between the football Cardinals and St. Louis. Throughout their 28 years in town, the "Big Red" often were high on potential but all too often disappointing in performance. During their entire St. Louis existence, they never hosted a postseason game. The franchise enjoyed a brief period of success in the mid-1970s. But the booster shot quickly wore off and by the 1980s, the pattern of mediocrity returned. Despite the offensive exploits of O.J. Anderson, Roy Green and Neil Lomax, the Cardinals won only 61 games and lost 89 in their final 10 years in St. Louis. In the meantime, Bidwill's complaints about the financial inadequacies of Busch Stadium grew louder. His demands for tax breaks and incentives became more serious, and as the 1987 season unfolded, it became evident the football Cardinals and Busch were on borrowed time. On Dec. 13, 1987, on an appropriately cold and blustery Sunday, the Big Red made their final appearance downtown. Although the impending move was not a done deal, the players and 29,623 fans in attendance recognized the handwriting on the concrete walls. And they were left with a warm, if melancholy, memory: The Cardinals beat the New York Giants 27-24. When the game ended, the crowd acknowledged the moment by singing a chorus of "Na na na na… hey, hey, hey, goodbye." Players responded by removing their helmets and raising them to the crowd as a final salute. "I love playing in St. Louis," running back Stump Mitchell said. "I don't want to leave." Eventually, the scene faded. The still of the evening enveloped Busch Stadium as a lonely figure remained fixed to his seat in Section 229. "I just wanted to sit here awhile when everyone else was gone," the bearded man said. "I just wanted to remember. There's a lot of nostalgia here; there's a lot of my life here." So he sat there, and he cried. ∎

The football Cards of the 1980s all too often put a frown on the face of coach Jim Hanifan.

MOMENTS

"I always told myself if I ever got to the point where I couldn't maintain that level of play, either through old age or bad knees, I wouldn't try to kid myself into thinking I could keep playing. I wouldn't try to fool the coaching staff and I wouldn't try to fool Mr. Bidwill.

"... I've had all the accolades and pats on the back that one human can normally tolerate without becoming an egomaniac. I have no regrets."

— Future Hall of Famer Dan Dierdorf, announcing his retirement at a Stadium Club press conference

Fans at Busch Stadium say goodbye to the Cardinals' Dan Dierdorf before the final game of the Hall of Fame tackle's 13-year career on Dec. 18, 1983.

MOMENTS

"1986, that was a bad football Cardinals team (is that redundant?). I remember returning from a weekend visit back home in New York to hurry over to Busch Stadium for a game. It was late in the year and we were leading the great Washington Redskins before they struck for two quick touchdowns and an eventual 20-17 loss for the Big Red.

"If that wasn't bad enough, I went out to my car after the game to find out the trunk was broken into and my luggage was stolen. And so it goes for a football Cardinals fan."

— **Roger J. Drake,
New Hyde Park, N.Y.**

Another Sunday, another pounding for quarterback Neil Lomax — this time at the hands of Washington's Darryl Grant in a 1983 game at Busch.

Ottis "O.J." Anderson squeezes through the Eagles in a 1984 game. Anderson rushes for a franchise-record 7,999 yards from 1979-86, but when the Big Red start 0-5 in '86, he's traded to the New York Giants for two draft picks.

Grocery bags on the heads of spectators in 1986 are a sign of how far the Cardinals had fallen. The Big Red finish 4-11-1 that season.

MOMENTS

"I needed a 70,000-seat stadium to compete in the NFL, and no one wanted to do it in St. Louis. They thought that Busch Stadium was perfectly adequate. It wasn't. The NFL agreed with me, and we moved.

"We had a good run in St. Louis, and I was very happy there — it's a great place to live. I miss going to lunch at the Stadium Club or Crown Candy. I have no problem with the football fans in St. Louis. I think they are good sports fans.

"We liked St. Louis. If they'd built a new building for us, we'd still be there. That was St. Louis' choice, not mine."

— William V. "Bill" Bidwill, owner of the NFL's Cardinals

After the 1987 season, Cardinals owner Bill Bidwill closes the books on 28 seasons in St. Louis and moves the Big Red to Arizona.

The Stones roll in

August - September 1989

With a venue that seated more than 50,000 people, concerts were never about quantity at Busch Stadium, they were about quality. And two of the most memorable musical events at the ballpark took place within weeks of each other in 1989. When the Who came to the downtown rotunda on Aug. 11, 1989, more than 50,000 came to see Roger Daltrey, Pete Townshend and John Entwistle perform rock classics such as "My Generation" and "Won't Get Fooled Again." A 12-piece band accompanied the original members of the Who on a stage built between the left- and right-field bleachers. During the "Tommy" medley, a giant silver "pinball" balloon was released to roll and bounce among the crowd. Five weeks later, on Sept. 17, 1989, the Rolling Stones took the stadium by storm, appearing in St. Louis for the first time since a 1978 show at Kiel Auditorium. The "Steel Wheels" tour featured $2\frac{1}{2}$ hours of Mick Jagger, Keith Richards and company rocking through 27 of the band's biggest hits, from "Start Me Up" to "Satisfaction." More than 52,000 surrounded a huge

Mick Jagger and Ron Woods perform as the Rolling Stones' "Steel Wheels" tour hits Busch Stadium on Sept. 17, 1989.

center-field stage — 300 feet wide by 120 feet tall — that was created to resemble a railroad car. The evening ended with a fireworks display over the stadium. Mike Herman, 42, came from Little Rock, Ark. to see the Stones at Busch. He estimated he had seen the "world's greatest rock and roll band" more than 20 times. "The Stones have such mass appeal," Herman said. "Their music has never gotten old ... I always tell people that a Stones concert is not a concert, it's a happening. You can go to a million concerts, but you'll always remember a Stones show." Remembrances made for good business at Busch. Some concession stands reportedly had earned close to $15,000 just one hour into the concert, selling T-shirts at $20 to $35 apiece. ∎

On a stage set up between Busch Stadium's left-field and right-field bleachers, the Who plays to a packed house on Aug. 11, 1989.

The Cardinals' Big Eagle

MOMENTS

"When he was in better health, he would leave the office at Anheuser-Busch and walk to Busch Stadium.

"It was like a parade. People would follow him, pat him on the back, shake his hand. He especially loved it when the kids asked for his autograph."

— Alfred Fleishman, public relations adviser to "Gussie" Busch

There have been Hall of Fame players, unforgettable broadcasters and rabid fans too many to count. But no figure stands out more distinctly in Busch Stadium history than "Gussie." August A. Busch Jr., the gravel-voiced beer baron, philanthropist and sportsman, was a driving force behind the building of the downtown stadium. With his guileless personality and competitive fire, he was the patriarch of Cardinals baseball from 1953 until his death Sept. 29, 1989, at age 90. Opening day and postseason tradition in the 1980s called for the Cardinals' crusty owner to don a red cowboy hat, sit atop the Budweiser beer wagon and guide the brewery's famous Clydesdales into the stadium. The Budweiser theme, "Here Comes the King," became the official song of baseball in St. Louis. Busch preferred boating, hunting and horses to baseball, but his zeal for the Cardinals was uncompromising, and his temper was legendary. He once kicked a hole in the wall of his private box at Busch Stadium after a defeat. Before the advent of free agency, "The Big Eagle" was known for treating his players well — he made Stan Musial the first $100,000-a-year ballplayer — and placed a high premium on their loyalty. When the major league

Cardinals owner Gussie Busch is not averse to a little finger-pointing when his team reaches the playoffs in 1982.

players struck in 1972, he was deeply hurt. "Let them strike," he said. "I won't give them one more damned cent." After the strike ended, Busch angrily ordered general manager Bing Devine to trade two of his young pitchers, Steve Carlton and Jerry Reuss, because of their salary demands. But when it became evident baseball's new economic order was here to stay, Busch made it known he would do "whatever it takes" to win. In 1980, without a pennant since 1968, he hired Whitey Herzog as field manager, and later general manager, trusting "The Rat" could lead his franchise back to prominence. When Herzog's retooled team won the 1982 World Series, Busch was ecstatic in a champagne-soaked clubhouse and uttered his traditional pennant-winning refrain: "I've never been happier in my whole life." ∎

The success of the Cardinals in the '80s helps make owner August A. Busch Jr. a fan favorite, especially when he rides into the stadium behind a team of Clydesdales.

MOMENTS

"A couple weeks after I took over (in 1980), Gussie called me up to his office in Busch Stadium and growled, 'Well, what have I got?'

" 'Well, Chief, you've got a bunch of prima donnas. You've got a bunch of mean people, some sorry human beings. It's the first time I've ever been scared to walk through my own clubhouse.'

" 'You really think it's that bad?' Gussie said.

" 'We ain't going to win with this sorry bunch. We've got to do some housecleaning.'

" 'Well,' Gussie said, 'keep me posted.' "

— Whitey Herzog, describing his working relationship with Gussie Busch, in his autobiography "White Rat"

Only two years after Gussie Busch hires Whitey Herzog to win a championship, they reach their goal with a World Series title in 1982.

RIGHT: Busch's death on Sept. 29, 1989, at age 90 brings a moment of silence for manager Whitey Herzog, his team and the Busch Stadium crowd.

The
1990s

BY DAN O'NEILL OF THE POST-DISPATCH

The most turbulent times in the history of Busch Stadium occurred in the 1990s, a decade marked by dramatic events and, ultimately, a spirited rebirth. After appearing in three World Series in the 1980s and coming close to another division title in 1989, the Cardinals withdrew in the early part of the decade. Anheuser-Busch Cos. Inc. and chairman August A. Busch III became increasingly resistant to the escalating salaries and financial parameters of the game, and the product on the field retreated into mediocrity. The transition came to a head when Whitey Herzog resigned as the club's manager on July 6, 1990. The organization turned to old friend Joe Torre, who had won the National League MVP award as a Cardinal in 1971 and eagerly took the task. "To come back here and put on the Cardinal uniform again, I can't tell you what that does to me," Torre said. "I have goose bumps. St. Louis has always been a second home to me, and now it's my first home." But the success he would realize later in New York did not materialize in St. Louis. Over the next five years, three of his teams finished with winning records, but none seriously contended for a division crown.

Mark McGwire caps off an unforgettable 1998 season with two home runs in the final game, including his record-setting 70th.

MOMENTS

"What gave me the biggest kick? The crowd. I never saw a situation where people got on their feet and stayed on their feet for every at-bat.

"The commotion he causes. The gasp when he swings and misses. The din when he hits a popup. People checking their scorecard to see when you go to the concession stand or the bathroom. You don't want to miss him hit.

"He controls everything at the ballpark. Ticket sales. Parking. The size of the crowd. It all revolves around him.

"We draw 3.2 million fans but finish 20 games out of the pennant race. And I see a lot more kids at the ball-park in September, when school starts, than I ever did before."

— **Jack Buck,
on Mark McGwire's
70-homer season in 1998**

The darkest baseball moment of the decade, however, had nothing to do with Torre. On Aug. 12, 1994, major league players walked off the job as negotiations for a new collective bargaining agreement broke down. A few weeks later, on Sept. 14, the baseball heart of the city stopped beating altogether when the remainder of the season was officially canceled. "The game is going to suffer," said Bing Devine, a former Cardinals general manager and a native St. Louisan. "The game will come back; fans will come back. But it won't be as easy, and they won't come back as quickly as in the past. But they will come back."

The game did come back in April 1995, when a federal judge issued an injunction against major league owners. But Torre came back only briefly. When the Cardinals got off to a 20-27 start, management fired Torre and named Mike Jorgensen the interim manager. The true repercussions of the change began when the club introduced Tony La Russa as its new manager on Oct. 10, 1995. The arrival of La Russa signaled a new era in Cardinals history. And to that end, the most significant news was just days away.

On Oct. 25, 1995, citing operating losses of $12 million for the '95 season, Anheuser-Busch made the stunning announcement it was selling the Cardinals. Just like that, a 42-year relationship that included six pennants, three world championships, several Hall of Famers, teams of Clydesdales, Gussie Busch's red cowboy hat and crowds swaying to the Budweiser theme song flashed before St. Louis' eyes. Less than two months later, a group of investors

Greg Cissell of the Webster Groves Marching Statesmen puts his heart and lungs into a trumpet solo at the 1994 Greater St. Louis Marching Band Festival in Busch Stadium.

with strong local ties announced it had purchased the team and the stadium for $150 million.

Baseball wasn't the only sport making radical news in town. On April 12, 1995, the National Football League approved the transfer of the Los Angeles Rams franchise to St. Louis. A key component in securing the team was the lure of a $280 million domed stadium.

However, the new digs weren't ready for prime time when the 1995 NFL season began, so on Sept. 10, 1995, the Rams made their St. Louis debut at an old haunt — Busch Stadium. More than 58,000 fans roared with approval as professional football

ST. LOUIS MOMENTS

1990	1991	1992	1993	1994
Schools close, emergency drills are held, medical supplies are stockpiled — all because climatologist Iben Browning predicts an earthquake in the St. Louis region for Dec. 1-5.	Rocker Axl Rose jumps into the crowd and ignites a riot at the Guns 'N' Roses concert at Riverport Amphitheatre; 75 people are injured.	Post-Dispatch investigation discloses that George Peach, chief prosecutor in St. Louis, has been using public money to pay for sex for a decade.	The Great Flood inundates 300 businesses in Chesterfield Valley and turns communities into watery ghost towns. By Aug. 1, Mississippi hits its highest level ever recorded.	Kiel Center opens as the new home for the Blues, but with the players locked out in a labor dispute, the arena's first event is an NBA exhibition game.

Busch Stadium takes on a blue hue as the St. Louis Rams play their first home game, ending the city's eight-year drought without professional football.

1995
The Belleville Diocese wraps up its investigation of child sexual abuse by priests; 13 priests and one deacon are removed.

1996
After weathering a 99-day strike by 6,700 machinists, McDonnell Douglas announces a merger with Boeing to create the world's largest aircraft company.

1997
Freeman Bosley Jr., the first black mayor of St. Louis, loses his re-election bid after a term plagued by scandals.

1998
DNA tests reveal that remains from Vietnam War in the Tomb of the Unknowns in Washington are those of Michael Blassie, who is brought home to St. Louis for a hero's burial.

1999
Pope John Paul II visits St. Louis and celebrates Mass before 104,000 people at the Trans World Dome and America's Center.

Elton John sports a red leather suit for his Aug. 9, 1994 show with Billy Joel at Busch. According to the Post-Dispatch, the Brit and the American manage to "turn the gigantic, impersonal stadium into an intimate piano lounge, mesmerizing the 50,000 or so in attendance."

years of artificial turf, the playing surface was restored to natural grass. The return to terra firma signaled the conversion of Busch from a multipurpose past to a baseball-specific future. Early in the 1990s, Busch staged well-attended concerts by groups such as New Kids on the Block and U2, and even a World Wrestling Federation event during Hulk Hogan's heyday. Former Beatle Paul McCartney returned to the ballpark with a solo concert in 1993. Even later in the '90s, Busch had its unorthodox moments, such as 1997, when Steve Fossett twice launched hot-air balloons from the ballpark in failed attempts to fly around the globe.

But the mid-'90s adaptation to real grass made it clear baseball was the stadium's bread and butter, and additional changes complemented the theme. A hand-operated scoreboard was constructed in center field's upper deck, resplendent with commemorative flags honoring world championships and retired numbers. Busch Stadium never looked older, and never looked better.

The embellishments made a wholesome backdrop for the spectacular events of 1998, aka the "Summer of 70." Mark McGwire and Sammy Sosa staged a home run race that filled ballparks throughout the land and erased the ugly residue of the strike of '94. Although the Cardinals finished 19 games out of first place, McGwire's swat watch pushed stadium attendance over 3 million.

On Sept. 8, 1998, with Sosa patrolling right field for the visiting Chicago Cubs, with 49,987 flashbulb-popping patrons in the stands, McGwire hit his 62nd homer to break Roger Maris' single-season home run record of 61. "Big Mac" capped his season by hitting eight more homers, cracking No. 70 on the final day of the season at Busch Stadium. McGwire's mark stood only two full seasons. But for those who witnessed the Summer of 70 at Busch Stadium, it was the summer of a lifetime. ∎

returned with the St. Louis Rams' 17-13 victory over the New Orleans Saints. The Rams played four games at Busch before moving to the Trans World Dome, the last on Oct. 22, 1995, before a record gathering of 59,915.

The decade wasn't just about changes affecting residents of the stadium; it brought major alterations to the facility as well. Before the 1995 baseball season, the Plaza of Champions display, featuring monuments to past heroes and championship teams, was erected near the Stan Musial statue.

In 1996, the new owners wasted little time in giving their 30-year-old "cookie cutter" ballpark a more traditional look. After 26

RIGHT: Ozzie Smith waves goodbye to the Busch faithful on Ozzie Smith Appreciation Day, Sept. 28, 1996. A reservation at Cooperstown awaited him five years down the road.

No joy in Buschville

Summer 1994

MOMENTS

So foul a sky,
Shakespeare wrote, clears
not without a storm.
And so it was at cheerless
250 Stadium Plaza.

In a rude irony, dozens of
fans from hundreds of miles
away were pinned against
impenetrable Busch Stadium
during a thunderstorm that
effectively trumpeted the
state of the game.

Kathy Young of Austin,
Texas, and her two children
had planned their summer
around a trip to see the
Cardinals. Her son Daniel, 15,
was crestfallen. Instead of
watching the Cards vs. the
Phillies, they were relegated
to squinting through ramps
to the seats just to catch
patches of turf and tarps.

**— Post-Dispatch story about
the first day of the strike**

As former Cardinal and Hill neighborhood resident Joe Garagiola is wont to say: "Baseball is a funny game." But on Aug. 12, 1994, the fun stopped. Negotiations on a new collective bargaining agreement between owners and players had reached an impasse, so major league players packed their bags and went home, bringing a $2 billion industry to an abrupt halt just as pennant races were heating up. Just as it was with players' strikes in 1972 and '81, baseball fans such as Joan Frelich of Clayton got caught in the middle. "I'm a season-ticket holder and I am truly disgusted," she said. "As far as I'm concerned, it's greed, greed, greed on both sides. However, the players have no concern, no caring about the people who pay them their paychecks. And that, of course, is the fans." The news got worse before it got better. In mid-September, the commissioner's office canceled the World Series, which had been played for 89 consecutive years. "There cannot be any joy on any side," said acting commissioner Bud Selig. But Cardinals fans displayed their resiliency and loyalty just two weeks later when the Cardinals opened Busch

An announcement posted in the ticket lobby at Busch Stadium informs fans about a refund policy for tickets to games lost in the strike of 1994.

Stadium for Fan Appreciation Day. Nearly 50,000 baseball-hungry faithful turned out for on-field activities, $1 concessions and a chance to visit their home away from home. More than 18,000 hot dogs were sold. Several former Cardinals were there to sign autographs, as was manager Joe Torre. "It's incredible, but it's not surprising," Torre said. "Every single one of them has a smile on his face." The smiles were rewarded on April 2, 1995, when the owners accepted the players' offer to return to work. An abbreviated 144-game schedule was worked out, and the Cardinals opened their home portion with a 7-6 victory over the Phillies on April 26. Still, the residual strike damage was evident the following day when only 13,483 showed up for a "Businessman's Special." ■

The Cardinals clubhouse sits empty in September 1994, with a strike having wiped out the end of the season and the World Series.

One last football fling

September 1995

When the football Cardinals ditched St. Louis after the 1987 season, it appeared Busch Stadium had seen the last of professional football, one of its primary tenants. But in the business of franchise transfers, one good move deserves another. With the lure of a sweetheart deal that included a $280 million domed stadium on the north side of downtown, the Los Angeles Rams said goodbye to Hollywood in 1995 and hello to the Gateway City. However, as the St. Louis Rams prepared to open their inaugural season, delays put their new stadium on hold. So a football-famished gathering of 59,335 returned to the scene of the crime – at least that's how some felt about the Big Red leaving – and welcomed the NFL back to Busch Stadium on Sept. 10, 1995. "We are starved," said Ron Uelk of St. Charles, munching on a pre-game bratwurst. "Starved for football, I mean. You have to remember, it's been eight years without a team. We have missed this a lot." The Rams made the home-coming a success, beginning a new era with a 17-13 victory over the New Orleans Saints. The two became fast friends, the new team and the old stadium. While finishing touches continued to be applied to the Dome, the houseguests continued to soak up the great outdoors. A crowd of 59,679 fans whooped it up Sept. 24 as the Rams came from behind to beat the Chicago Bears 34-28, improving their record to 4-0 overall and 3-0 in St. Louis. "Why leave Busch?" quarterback Chris Miller said. "The crowds have been fantastic. Let's see if we can go undefeated there." But the flourishing affiliation between the Rams and Busch Stadium ended with a thud. A Busch-record crowd of 59,915 filled the seats Oct. 22 for what would be the final NFL game there. Many left early as the San Francisco 49ers pounded the Rams 44-10. Less than a month later, the town's newest sports toy opened its new stadium, and Busch Stadium fell football-silent once more. ∎

MOMENTS

"The fans were so responsive, so loving. I was just overwhelmed with it.

"I wanted to cry, but I couldn't find my waterproof mascara."

— **Rams owner and native St. Louisan Georgia Frontiere, after her team's debut at Busch Stadium**

Owner Georgia Frontiere's prayers are answered as the Rams win their home opener 17-13 over the Saints. Joining Frontiere on the sideline is Marshall Klein, the Rams' vice president of community relations.

With no shortage of fanfare, the Rams take the field at Busch Stadium and make it official: Football is back.

MOMENTS

"The moment that sticks out in my mind was the first Rams game back at Busch Stadium in 1995. It seems like we were all there in a state of disbelief, like we didn't REALLY have a team until we saw an official play.

"And when Jerome Bettis ran off-tackle for a 7-yard gain, Busch Stadium exploded! Louder than any moment I've ever heard at the Dome. The feeling was like, 'Finally! We have a football team again.'"

— **St. Louisan Brian Rouse**

Second-year wide receiver Isaac Bruce hauls in a pass for a 53-yard gain against San Francisco in the Rams' final game at Busch, shortly before Bruce took his considerable skills down the street to the new domed stadium.

Eight years of bottled-up football passion burst forth with the Rams' debut at Busch.

New owners, new era

Summer 1996

The notion had drifted through town in gossip form, the rumor variety of an urban legend. But when the official announcement came, few headlines in recent St. Louis history have been more stunning than the one that ran across the top of Page A1 of the Post-Dispatch on Oct. 25, 1995: "Busch, Cards breaking up/ Brewery to sell team." The news that Anheuser-Busch was ending its 42-year relationship with the Cardinals knocked the air out of the local sports community. The words of Marge Schott, president of the Cincinnati Reds, reflected a national astonishment. "This makes me sick to my stomach," Schott said. "Are we going to have no family ownerships left in baseball?" The unsettling situation, the fear of the unknown, dissipated soon enough when a new ownership group stepped to the forefront two months later. These men wore Cardinal-red hearts on their sleeves and used words that were melodious to a region of disoriented Cardinals fans. "We want to win now," said Frederick O. Hanser, who was introduced as chairman of the group. "The fans deserve to see some more World Series and some championships." The change of ownership coincided with changes on and off the field. With football no longer a primary tenant, the "multipurpose" stadium was made over to present a cozier, more traditional baseball atmosphere. The highlights: installation of a natural grass playing surface for the first time in 26 years, a family pavilion in left field, a picnic area in left-center field and new sections that put fans closer to the action all around the park. All improvements were in place for the 1996 season, as was a dramatic improvement on the field. The Cardinals won the National League Central title, making it to postseason play for the first time since 1987. With Mark McGwire's assault on the single-season home run record, the Cardinals topped the 3 million mark in attendance in 1998 and repeated the feat in 1999. ∎

By late December 1995, the Cardinals franchise is firmly in the mitts of new owners. From left are Bill DeWitt Jr., Fred Hanser and Andrew Baur.

As it approaches its 30th birthday, the stadium gets a face-lift in February 1996 as grass is reintroduced after a 26-year absence.

If not a pot of gold, the Cardinals find a division title at the end of the rainbow in 1996, Tony La Russa's first season as their manager.

MOMENTS

"The fans at Busch Stadium are really in the game. It's the way baseball ought to be. It's the way it ought to be in St. Louis one month every year, bringing back the memories."

— Cards outfielder Brian Jordan, as postseason baseball returned in 1996

Although a Game 4-winning homer by Brian Jordan isn't enough to carry the Cardinals past Atlanta in the 1996 NLCS, the stadium is home to winning baseball again.

McGwire leaves a mark

September 8, 1998

MOMENTS

"By far the greatest moment was when McGwire went into the seats at Busch Stadium after he hit No. 62 and embraced the Marises. It told us a lot about what Mark McGwire was about. And it also told us a lot about what baseball is about at its best.

"Only in baseball would something like that happen. Only in baseball would it make perfect sense. The linking of generations is not a footnote. It's at the heart of the game.

"And that's something that is unique to baseball."

— St. Louisan Bob Costas

It began as spring-training speculation in 1998, grew into a summer phenomenon and eventually infatuated the nation. It began with Mark McGwire hitting a grand slam on opening day and ended with baseball's place in the public conscience restored. On Tuesday, Sept. 8, 1998, with 49,987 in the stands at Busch Stadium, with flashbulbs popping like Fourth of July sparklers, with the Cubs leading 2-0 in the fourth inning and pitcher Steve Trachsel on the mound, with 8:18 p.m. showing on the stadium clock and with the first pitch, McGwire pulled a drive down the third-base line that traveled 341 feet and 37 years. The home run was McGwire's 62nd of the season, which exceeded Roger Maris' record of 61 homers in 1961. And the scene was unlike any other in Busch Stadium history. McGwire began his historic trot by initially missing first base in his exuberance. He jumped into the arms of first base coach Dave McKay. He slapped hands and accepted congratulations from Cubs infielders as he made his way around the bases. He tapped his chest and pointed to the sky as he approached home plate, letting Maris know he was in his heart. As he arrived at home, the 34-year-old first baseman lifted and hugged his son Matthew, who was serving as the Cardinals bat boy. He hugged his teammates. He hugged and exchanged salutes with Cubs outfielder Sammy Sosa, his adversary in baseball's most memorable home run race, his soul mate at that record-breaking moment. McGwire then climbed into a section of box seats to embrace members of the Maris family, who had come to St. Louis to sanction his accomplishment. In all, the midgame pageantry lasted more than 11 minutes. In all likelihood, there wasn't a dry eye in the house. "I sure the heck was floating," McGwire said. "I hope I didn't act foolish, but this was history." ■

The sight of Mark McGwire loosening up in the on-deck circle is enough to unsettle opposing pitchers throughout the 1998 season.

Ryan Klippel (left) and Phillip Hunt watch the ball hit the Stadium Club in left field on Mark McGwire's 25th homer of the '98 season.

MOMENTS

They are giving us quite a show, Mark McGwire and Sammy Sosa. They are giving us thrills, drama and mid game bulletins.

More than anything, McGwire and Sosa are giving us the best of themselves. As the home run totals mount, the suspense builds, but their eyes light up, wider and brighter. Mac and Sammy are taking the pressure, and shoving it out of the way, so they can entertain America with their big smiles and bigger bats.

They are having a duel but continue to laugh through it, spreading good cheer and good sportsmanship.

— Columnist Bernie Miklasz, writing for the Post-Dispatch in 1998

For the Cubs' Sammy Sosa and the Cardinals' Mark McGwire, the race to break Roger Maris' home run record is a friendly competition.

Mark McGwire's monstrous shots in batting practice become a phenomenon in 1998, attracting visiting players as well as fans and teammates.

MOMENTS

"Every time McGwire swung back then, the stadium lit up with flashes from thousands of cameras. The crowd focused on every move he made. Me? I was just eating pizza and chatting away with my dad.

"Then McGwire swung, the ball was sailing to left field … and it dropped over the wall! The crowd erupted! I did, too, and as my hands flew up in the air, the slice of pizza sailed away and landed about four rows down — on the bald head of another Cardinals fan.

"He spun around to look for the 'assailant' — a slice of pizza sitting on his head — but I locked in on McGwire as he rounded the bases. No. 62 remains one of the funniest moments of my life."

— **Jonathan Lane, Ballwin, Mo.**

A slow-shutter exposure captures some of the camera flashes on Sept. 8, 1998, as fans hope to record McGwire's 62nd home run.

RIGHT: Catching a McGwire home run ball is serious competition. Jason Bolton of Rochester, Mich., positions himself to catch No. 68. "The ball was in my glove, then popped out," he lamented.

With each hug from his father after a historic home run, Matthew McGwire becomes an integral part of the celebration at the stadium. This homer is McGwire's 61st, hit on his father's 61st birthday.

MOMENTS

"I never knew how I'd feel, but it was an awesome feeling. To tell you the truth, I've wanted him to hit 62 all along. ... I'm in love with the guy, but I wanted to see him earn it.

"So I'm just glad he did it against the Cubs, so no one can say, 'Well, they threw him a gopher ball, they just lobbed it in there for him.' The Cubs weren't going to give anything to him, because of Sosa and the pennant race."

— Roger Maris Jr.,
who sat in a Busch Stadium box seat next to the Cardinals dugout as Mark McGwire hit No. 62

After seeing his father's home run record tied, a tearful Randy Maris visits with Mark McGwire.

161

MOMENTS

"Swing and a shot into the
corner. It might make it!
There it is: 62, folks!
It just got over the left-
field wall in the corner.
And we have a new
home run champion!
A new Sultan of Swat!
It's Mark McGwire!
He touches them all.
Unbelievable."

**— Mike Shannon,
calling No. 62 on KMOX**

"Down the line. Is it enough?
G-O-O-O-NE! There it is!
Sixty-two! Touch first, Mark.
You are the new single-
season home run king."

**— Joe Buck,
calling No. 62 on Fox TV**

When No. 62 leaves the park on Sept. 8, 1998, baseball has a new home run king.

RIGHT: Mark McGwire's trip around the bases after his 62nd homer — one of Busch Stadium's finest moments.
"It was a sweet, sweet run," he said.

MOMENTS

With a crack of the bat, Mark McGwire sent a wicked streak of lightning through the night sky over St. Louis — a thunderbolt to the baseball gods. He would be joining them now.

"Thanks to Babe, Roger and everybody who's watching up there," McGwire said.

The baseball icons on this earth were mighty impressed, too. Stan Musial, Ozzie Smith, Lou Brock were on their feet at Busch Stadium, laughing and clapping. McGwire was one of them now, a Cardinal of legendary distinction.

The magical moment immediately became one of the most important questions in St. Louis history: Where were you when No. 62 went out?

— **Post-Dispatch columnist Bernie Miklasz**

An awestruck McGwire watches as his 62nd homer is replayed on the video scoreboard.

RIGHT: Fireworks light the sky over Busch Stadium after No. 62.

Events for all reasons

With the loss of the football Cardinals after 1987, stadium proprietors entertained alternative ways to keep Busch both active and financially viable through the 1990s. True to its original "multipurpose" theme, the ballpark became a community playhouse of sorts, especially before the reintroduction of a grass field. Conventional staples, such as high school and college sports, continued to be part of the lineup. The Gateway Classic, a football game for teams from historically black colleges, began a three-year run at Busch in 1993 with a wildly entertaining game between Alcorn State and victorious Howard University. But the stadium also stretched its facilitating wings, embracing events both public and private, from Steve Fossett's hot-air balloon launches to high school graduations and proms. A good example of the "outside the box" programs was the WWF Wrestlefest on July 14, 1991. An animated crowd saw The Ultimate Warrior defeat the Undertaker in a casket match and Hulk Hogan pin Sgt. Slaughter. The latter match even had a guest referee with ties to the Cardinals — former minor leaguer Randy Poffo, who had repackaged himself as WWF superstar Randy "Macho Man" Savage. Also in the 1990s, Busch continued its long run as site for the

Twenty-seven years after his performance at Busch with the Beatles, Paul McCartney revisits in 1993.

Greater St. Louis Marching Band Festival. The spongy artificial turf was different from the dirt fields the high school ensembles were used to practicing on. "It feels like you're marching on pillows," Monica Swindle of Northwest High said at the competition in 1994. The stadium continued to be the place for blockbuster concerts in St. Louis. The 1990s featured a few, such as U2, New Kids on the Block, Paul McCartney and Rock 'n' Country with Hank Williams Jr. But among the most memorable was an August 1994 show featuring Elton John and Billy Joel. The keyboard kings entertained more than 50,000 for 3 1/2 hours with 34 songs. ■

Steve Fossett's Solo Spirit lifts off on New Year's Eve, 1997, as the balloonist makes the second of his two launches from Busch Stadium in an effort to circumnavigate the world. Although both attempts failed, Fossett later achieved his goal.

MOMENTS

Early Sunday afternoon at Busch Stadium, the New Kids on the Block weren't even in the neighborhood, but try telling that to adoring teen-age girls toting hand-lettered posters, all in homage to their beloved Kids. Gaggles of girls peered into every taxi that passed by the stadium and shrieked at the sight of a limo two blocks away.

The cause of all this adolescent hysteria? The New Kids on the Block were in St. Louis as part of their "Magic Summer" tour. ... A sell-out crowd of 49,000 emitted a deafening chorus of squeals when the band finally took the stage at 8:40 p.m. The screams continued during every song, every dance move.

About 50 people were treated for injuries. Most of those were youngsters who became overheated and overexcited.

— **Post-Dispatch archives**

Three fans from Brighton, Ill., can't wait until the Busch Stadium gates open for the New Kids on the Block concert on Aug. 26, 1990. From left, Linnetta Lowder, 11; Marcie Lowder, 11; and Karen Lowder, 8.

The Troy Buchanan Marching Band warms up on Oct. 21, 1995, the final appearance at the stadium for the Greater St. Louis Marching Band Festival before its move to the new domed stadium downtown.

The
2000s

BY DAN O'NEILL OF THE POST-DISPATCH

Baseball and Busch Stadium were joined at the hip as St. Louis ushered in the new millennium. And as the collaboration ran its course, as the stadium that helped resurrect the franchise and resuscitate downtown acquiesced to the new stadium emerging next door, the partnership enjoyed some of its finest hours. The Cardinals won four pennants and three World Series titles in the 1940s; no decade in their history has been more eventful. But in the first half of the new millennium's first decade, the franchise experienced significant highs, painful lows and its most consistent run of success in 60 years. Manager Tony La Russa ingratiated himself to a town that was slow to embrace him and solidified his place of significance in Cardinals lore. General manager Walt Jocketty made bold acquisitions that kept the Cardinals at the top of the class. Albert Pujols emerged as an elite player in the game, building platforms for a Hall of Fame career. And to soak it all in, fans went through the turnstiles in unprecedented numbers.

In one of the highlights of the 2004 postseason, the Cardinals wait to mob Jim Edmonds at home plate after his game-winning home run in the 12th inning of Game 6 in the National League Championship Series. The victory ties the series 3-3, and the Cardinals win Game 7 to advance to the World Series.

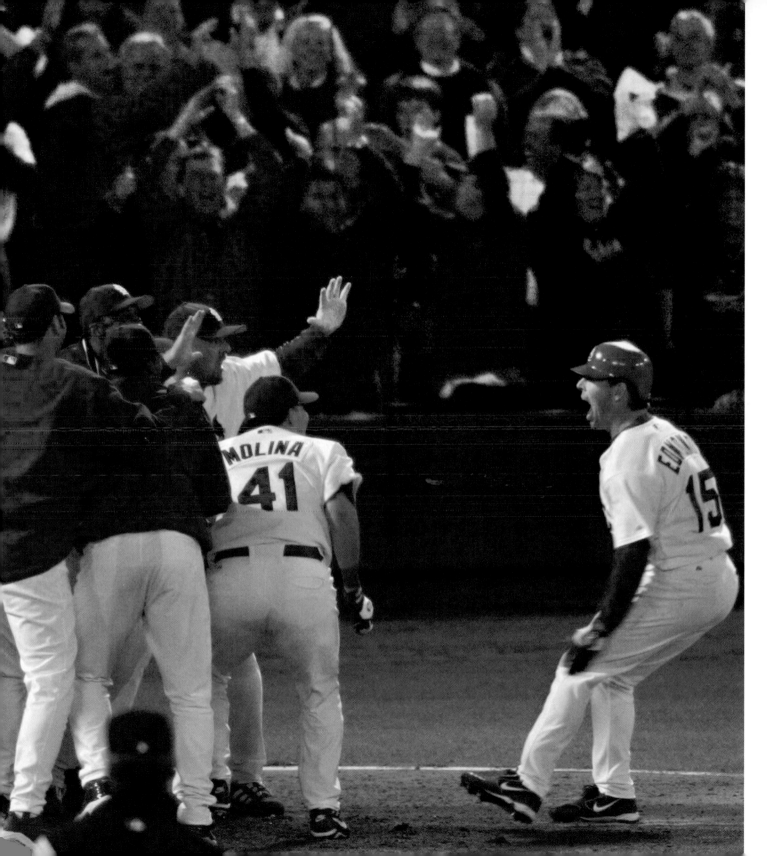

MOMENTS

"Everyone in the stadium was standing and cheering as the bottom of the 12th came. My chest felt tight. I couldn't watch. I couldn't breathe. But I felt lucky to be in the moment, lucky to be in Busch Stadium, to be part of the 50,000 who turned it into a screaming sea of red.

"I heard the crack from Edmonds' bat. ... I didn't watch the ball. I watched Edmonds. When I saw him do his stand-and-stare routine, then flip his bat and pump his fists, I just screamed. I just knew that Edmonds had lifted himself into the great moments of Cardinals history.

"We were goofy with joy, goofy all the way down the ramps, and into the streets. People were screaming, stomping their feet, honking horns. Rarely have I felt so alive as being a part of that electrifying crowd."

— Cardinals fan Beth Lewis

171

Despite his leg braces, 8-year-old Kyle Waelterman heads for home at one of the "Run the Bases" promotions that were popular in the latter years of Busch Stadium. His father, Todd, pushes Kyle's wheelchair.

"I'm proud of what we've been able to do over the past few seasons," La Russa said. "There have been disappointments because we haven't won it all. But I'm proud of the way we have gone about it and the way we have competed year in and year out."

After three seasons (1997-99) of also-ran frustration, La Russa's Cardinals captured a National League Central title in 2000, winning 95 games and outdistancing Cincinnati by a robust 10 games. The difference maker was center fielder Jim Edmonds, who was acquired from the Anaheim Angels just before spring training camp broke in late March.

Edmonds had a career year at the plate and also won a Gold Glove for his defense, something he would do annually in a Cardinals uniform. While Edmonds was the catalyst, Darryl Kile finished 20-9 on the mound, the club's first 20-game winner in more than a decade.

More than 52,000 came to Busch on Oct. 3 to see the Cardinals open the division series with a 7-5 victory over the Atlanta Braves, the first swoosh of a three-game sweep. But the momentum dissipated as the Cardinals dropped the NL Championship Series to New York in five games. During the same postseason, rookie pitching phenom Rick Ankiel experienced a baffling loss of control — he threw a record five wild pitches in one inning at Busch — from which he never fully recovered. Five years later, Ankiel gave up pitching to become an outfielder.

ST. LOUIS MOMENTS

2000
After a campaign stop in St. Louis on Oct. 16, Gov. Mel Carnahan dies in a plane crash near Hillsboro, Mo. His death occurs too late in the campaign for his name to be removed from the ballot, and Carnahan wins the election against incumbent Sen. John Ashcroft.

2001
St. Louis gets a bucketful of unwelcome national publicity when Alderman Irene Smith, who does not want to yield the floor during a debate, allegedly relieves herself in a trash can as fellow aldermen stand around her with sheets and blankets.

2002
Whoa, Nelly: The Grammy-winning rhymer who put St. Louis on the rap map is not allowed to enter Union Station because he is wearing a "do rag."

For Kylee Wagner of Charleston, Ill., there's no place like home plate for an exchange of vows with fellow Cardinals fan Jon Julius of Casey, Ill. On her wedding day in May 2005, she gets help with her dress from her maid of honor, Amanda Carr. Six couples say "I do" at Busch in the stadium's final summer.

2003

Lambert Field's run as a major airline hub ends as American Airlines cuts its flights in and out of the airport by half, eliminates nonstop flights to 27 cities and lays off 1,500 employees in St. Louis.

2004

FBI agents arrest Mike Danton of the Blues on charges that he tried to arrange the murder of his agent at Danton's apartment in Brentwood. Danton later pleads guilty and is sentenced to 7½ years in prison.

2005

Outsiders take over: Federated of Cincinnati buys May Co. and announces it will convert all Famous-Barr stores into Macy's. Lee Enterprises of Davenport, Iowa, buys Pulitzer Inc., ending 126 years of Post-Dispatch ownership by the Pulitzer family.

In a somber moment at Busch Stadium on Sept. 17, 2001, Jack Buck reads the poem he wrote after the terrorist attacks of 9/11. An excerpt:

With one voice we say, 'There is no choice today,
There is only one thing to do.'
Everyone is saying — the same thing — and praying
That we end these senseless moments we are living.
As our fathers did before ... we shall win this unwanted war.
And our children ... will enjoy the future ... we'll be giving.

The Cardinals repeated as NL Central champs in 2001, as Matt Morris won 22 games, Edmonds batted .304 with 110 RBIs, young outfielder J.D. Drew hit .323 with 27 homers and ... oh yeah, there was a rookie named Pujols.

Making the jump from Class A Peoria in one year, the 21-year-old Pujols made the club out of spring training and made himself a fixture in the Cardinals' future. He batted .329 with 37 home runs and 130 RBIs and was named the NL Rookie of the Year. All that excitement notwithstanding, the season ended prematurely as the Cards lost decisive Game 5 of the division series to Curt Schilling and the eventual World Series champion Arizona Diamondbacks.

The following year, the best baseball city in America became the saddest baseball city in America. On June 18, 2002, one of the most distinguished voices in sports history fell silent. Jack Buck, who had broadcast Cardinals games since 1954, who had been in the play-by-play booth at Busch Stadium since its inception, died at age 77 from a series of illnesses. On Thursday, June 20, more than 10,000 entered Busch Stadium to view Buck's casket and pay respects to the man who coined the phrase "That's a winner!"

None of those paying respect that day could have imagined that more heartbreak was to take place that weekend. On Saturday, June 22, as the Cardinals prepared to play the Chicago Cubs at Wrigley Field, Kile was found in his hotel room, dead at age 33. He had passed away in his sleep from a heart condition. On June 26, another memorial was held at Busch Stadium, this time for Kile. Along with friends, family, teammates and representatives from other major-league teams, 5,000 fans attended.

A place that had known so much happiness had become a place of mourning. Remarkably, La Russa held his team together. With Pujols collecting 34 homers and 127 RBIs, with the help of Jocketty's late-season acquisition of third baseman Scott Rolen, the Cardinals won 97 games and another NL Central crown. But the postseason bubble burst again.

Cardinals pitcher Darryl Kile relaxes on Father's Day with 9-month-old son Ryker and 5-year-old daughter Sierra at a father-child game on June 16, 2002. Six days later, Kile was found dead in his hotel room in Chicago.

While sweeping Arizona 3-0 in the division series, the Cardinals lost Rolen to an injury and then lost the NLCS in five games to Barry Bonds and the San Francisco Giants.

The string of postseason appearances was broken in 2003, despite a batting championship for Pujols, who hit .359, and a monstrous season by shortstop Edgar Renteria, who became the first shortstop in club history to reach 100 RBIs.

The best, however, was yet to come. With Pujols hitting .331 with 46 home runs, with Edmonds hitting 42 homers, with Rolen swatting 34 homers and collecting 124 RBIs, with four starters ringing up 15 or more victories, the Cardinals won 105 games in 2004. The victory total was the most for a Cardinals team since 1944.

The club defeated the Los Angeles Dodgers in the division series, then rallied from a 3-2 deficit to beat the Houston Astros in the NLCS. Edmonds won Game 6 with a home run in the bottom of the 12th, and Rolen's homer was the key blow in a dramatic Game 7 victory over Roger Clemens. As 52,140 danced out of their seats and into the streets around Busch Stadium, the Cardinals headed to their first World Series since 1987.

But the Fall Classic would belong to "Destiny's Darlings." In their quest to eradicate "the Curse of the Bambino" and end an 86-year drought without a championship, the Boston Red Sox swept the Cards in four games, clinching their long-sought title at Busch on Oct. 27, 2004.

Excitement echoed through the concrete corridors during one final summer as the Cardinals won their fourth division title in six seasons. A record number of spectators, more than 3.5 million, came through the gates of their sports home-away-from-home, hoping to say goodbye with one more world championship. But there would be no World Series do-over in 2005. The Astros brought the house down in Busch's final Octoberfest, winning an NLCS rematch in six games. ■

Eight-year-old Jim Tejcek and other Cardinals fans watch with concern as the Redbirds are losing 4-0 in the seventh inning of Game 3 of the 2004 World Series. Boston wins 4-1 on its way to a four-game sweep.

Cardinals center fielder Jim Edmonds puts his Gold Glove defense on display with a diving catch in Game 7 of the 2004 NLCS. Edmond's catch saves two runs and the Cards win 5-2 as Jeff Suppan outpitches Houston's Roger Clemens.

Tony earns his wings

2000-2005

MOMENTS

Brooding and grim, pacing and fidgeting in the dugout, with his hat brim pulled down. For public consumption, anyway, such is the demeanor of Tony La Russa. In addition to his calculating countenance, La Russa's monotone media voice and well-documented obsession with statistics lend further superficial evidence to evidence he is bloodless and robotic.

"I've always thought it would make a great book: 'The Anatomy of a Game,'" Cardinals chairman Fred Hanser said. "You could hook up the electrodes to him and go through every thought that went through his mind during a game. You'd learn a ton of a lot of baseball."

— Post-Dispatch archives

When he was hired before the 1996 season to manage the Cardinals, Tony La Russa had a track record. He had managed both the Chicago White Sox and the Oakland A's into the postseason, and had guided Oakland to a world championship. But when he was hired to manage the Cardinals, he was replacing personable Joe Torre, a former MVP as a Cardinal. He also was following Whitey Herzog, who had managed the club to a world championship and three pennants in the 1980s and had grown up in nearby New Athens, Ill. La Russa had credentials when he joined the Cardinals, but he had no following in St. Louis. "In Oakland, I had my time when I was popular with the people," said La Russa, who makes his home in the Bay area. "But this may be more important, because I came in here at zero." Over the next 10 seasons at Busch Stadium, La Russa earned that following and his place among the most significant managers in Cardinals history. The turning point in La Russa's public persona may have come in the 2002 season. In a span of just months, he lost his father, his god-father, a close friend and confidante in longtime

Manager Tony La Russa watched the Cardinals advance to the postseason in six of his 10 seasons at Busch Stadium.

Cardinals broadcaster Jack Buck and a clubhouse leader in pitcher Darryl Kile. The manner with which La Russa handled the grief and adversity, the strength with which he guided his team to another division title despite the emotional setbacks, helped win over even his most ardent detractors. "It was a difficult year, not just for me but for everybody connected to the organization," La Russa said. "Did I feel something from the fans? Like a lot of people, I'd say yes. Do I remember it? Yes." After leading the Cardinals to their first World Series appearance in 17 years, La Russa agreed to a three-year contract in December 2004. By the time the deal runs its course, he probably will be the winningest manager in franchise history, as well as a serious candidate for the Hall of Fame. Just as important, he is certain to leave St. Louis with a following. ∎

Tony La Russa sometimes bends over backwards to help his team win, which may explain why he's the third-winningest manager in baseball history.

MOMENTS

Steve Kline, outraged that he wasn't called into the game after warming up, slammed his glove to the bullpen ground and directed an obscene gesture toward his boss. When informed of Kline's tantrum, after the game, Tony La Russa's legendary temper flared.

"Give me two minutes," La Russa said, cutting off a live press conference, "and I'll be standing on top of his chest kicking the (bleep) out of him."

La Russa stomped into the shower room, where he found Kline in a different kind of lather. There La Russa dressed down the reliever before Kline could even dry off.

— Post-Dispatch coverage of a June 23, 2004 incident at Busch

Tony La Russa and outfielder So Taguchi honor the Cardinals' 2004 National League championship with a bow.

RIGHT: The spoils of victory include the traditional champagne shower, as outfielder Roger Cedeño douses Tony La Russa after the Cardinals finish off the Astros in the 2004 NLCS.

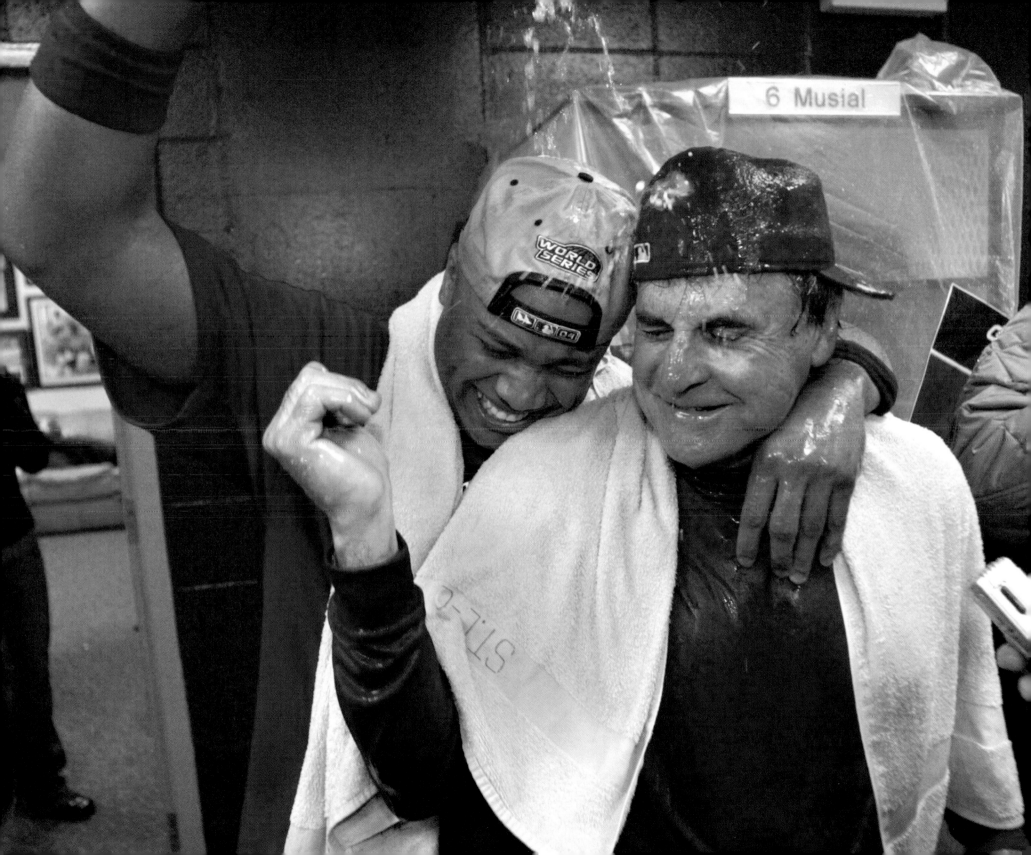

Great out of the gate

2001-2005

They come around once in a generation, if you're lucky. They leave a mark that is never erased, a foundation that anchors the teams they play on, a signature that defines the eras they play in. Rogers Hornsby was such a hitter; so was Stan Musial. And as the Cardinals flourished at the turn of the century, as Busch Stadium resonated with big crowds and baseball excitement, so was Albert Pujols. "He's as gifted a hitter as I've seen come along in a long, long time," Hall of Fame manager Sparky Anderson said. "Before he's done, we might be saying he's the best of them all." After making the leap from a Class A roster

After joining the Cardinals in 2001, Albert Pujols wasted no time in establishing himself as one of baseball's best hitters.

to the Cardinals lineup in spring 2001, Pujols batted .329 with 37 home runs and 130 runs batted in. But he was just getting started. He became the first player in major-league history to bat .300 or better with 30 or more homers, 100 or more RBIs and 100 or more runs scored in each of his first five seasons. In a poll of major-league players by Sports Illustrated in June 2005, Pujols was identified as the player most would build a team around. "He's unbelievable," teammate Larry Walker said. "He's not normal. He's a freak." In February 2004, the Cardinals signed Pujols to a seven-year deal worth an estimated $100 million. But the numbers that seemed to matter most to Pujols were found in the won-loss records. After another sizzling season in 2005, the Cardinals brought postseason play to Busch Stadium for the fourth time in Pujols' still blossoming five-year career. "I don't play the game for the numbers and the records," Pujols said. "I play to win. I play for my teammates. It doesn't matter what kind of numbers you put up if you don't win. I want a ring more than anything else. I want to share it with the guys in this clubhouse." ■

Albert Pujols makes a curtain call after a home run, a fairly common sight in the final years of Busch Stadium.

MOMENTS

A year ago, life was a little different for Albert Pujols. In his home opener for Class A Peoria, Pujols went hitless against the Beloit Snappers in front of 1,620 fans.

Now, let's fast-forward to his 2001 home opener ... He's a rookie for the St. Louis Cardinals. He's in the starting lineup, playing in front of a crowd of 48,702 at Busch Stadium. During pregame festivities, he's riding around the ring of the field in a convertible, waving to adoring fans.

In the second inning, he belts a shot over the wall for a two-run homer. Cardinal Nation goes berserk, screaming for Pujols to emerge from the dugout to acknowledge the sonic-boom applause. It's his first major-league curtain call.

— Post-Dispatch columnist Bernie Miklasz, describing Pujols' debut at Busch

No matter how you view him, Albert Pujols brings a heightened level of excitement to each trip to the plate.

For young Cardinals fans on Bat Day, it doesn't get much better than getting Albert Pujols' signature on their new lumber.

MOMENTS

"The best player I've ever managed is Albert Pujols. ... And what puts him over the top for me is that a big part of his motivation is winning the game that day.

"When you have a great player who is putting up huge numbers, but recognizing that this is a team competition, and all that matters is winning and losing, he goes right to the top. His No. 1 motivation as a player is coming to the ballpark each day determined to find a way to win."

— Cardinals manager Tony La Russa

Never afraid to play hard and get his uniform dirty, Albert Pujols chucks his helmet after being tagged out at home plate in a 2004 game against Houston.

MOMENTS

"People ask me if I believe how quickly my career has taken off. I just tell them Christ is my strength. God has blessed me and I will continue to do my best for Him. That is more important than anything I could ever do in baseball."

— Albert Pujols, speaking at a "Christian Family Day" program at Busch Stadium

As per his custom, Albert Pujols looks to the heavens after arriving at home plate on a home run.

MOMENTS

"Decades of memories prompted me to make a final, memorial trip to Busch Stadium on July 15, 2005. After the Astros broke a 2-2 tie in the 13th, I feared disappointment would cloud my final memory of Busch. Then, the most recent in a long line of Cardinals heroes saved the game with a two-run walk-off homer. I leaped to my feet with everyone else, cheered, clapped wildly ... then, reluctantly, took a final look around.

"My mind flooded with memories. Traveling to St. Louis as a teen to watch Bob Gibson, and sitting with my son years later as he watched his hero, Ozzie.

"Thank you, Albert Pujols, for the July 15 moment, and the promise of many memories to come in the new Busch Stadium."

— **Kay Schafer, Holmen, Wis.**

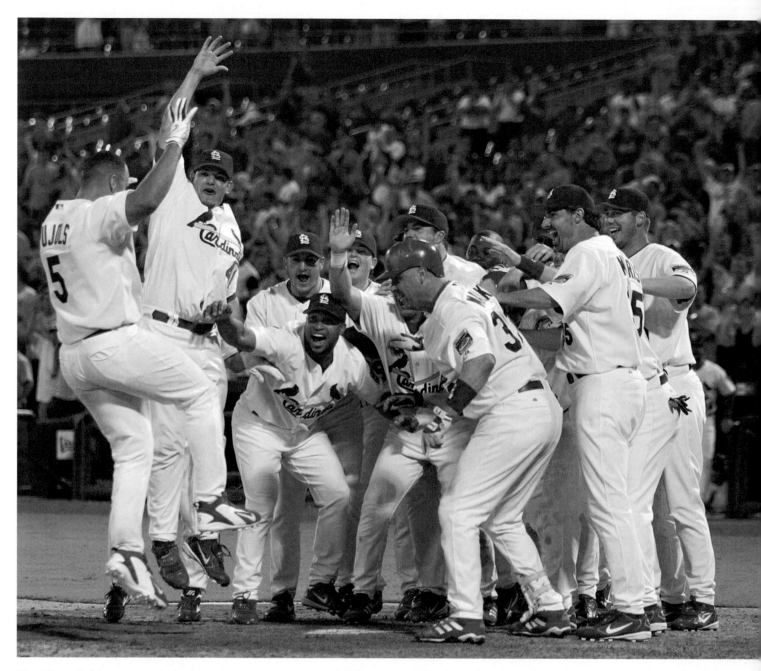

For Albert Pujols, some arrivals at home plate are more special than others. This home run gives the Cardinals a 13-inning victory over the Astros in July 2005.

As the sun sets on Busch Stadium in the summer of 2005, Albert Pujols offers Cardinals fans the promise of great seasons to come.

A place for mourning

June 2002

The site of so many thrills, a place of so much joy, Busch Stadium also became a place of reflection and mourning in the summer of 2002. First came the passing of Hall of Fame broadcaster Jack Buck, who started calling Cardinals games alongside Harry Caray in 1954. Not only were Buck's play-by-play descriptions unforgettable — "Go crazy, folks! Go crazy!" — but he became a treasured sports dinner personality and valued part of the community. Buck died June 18, 2002, at age 77, after a series of illnesses. Two days later, thousands came through the gates at Busch and filed past his casket to pay their respects. In a poignant service, Cardinals catcher Mike Matheny summed up the feelings of all in attendance by saying, "Mr. Buck, if I may borrow your words, pardon us while we stand and applaud." Two days later, on June 22, the baseball community got another jolt. Pitcher Darryl Kile, a 20-game winner in 2000, was found dead in his hotel room in Chicago moments before the Cardinals were to play at Wrigley Field. Kile, 33, died in his sleep of a heart attack. On June 26, the stadium so often covered in a "sea of red" once again was draped in black. Thousands of fans joined Kile's friends and family members for a memorial service near the mound, where he had stood so often. "This has been a hard week for St. Louis and the Cardinals," said Richard Gephardt, the congressman from St. Louis. "It's unimaginable that someone of (Kile's) age could die." The grieving created something of a phenomenon outside the stadium. The area around Jack Buck's statue became cluttered with flowers, pictures, posters and remembrances of Buck. Likewise, a corner area near the Cardinals offices became designated for Kile, and a similar sidewalk shrine emerged. One poster addressed both losses: "The heavens are bright, but the earth is darker. God has our two stars." ∎

The bust of Jack Buck outside Busch Stadium serves as a memorial after his death on June 18, 2002.

MOMENTS

"He's on another tier. It's like the president, the pope, the head of state, whatever you want to call it.

"It's like losing somebody like that."

— Cards outfielder Jim Edmonds, after the memorial service for Jack Buck at Busch Stadium

Jack Buck's headset sits in the KMOX broadcast booth overlooking the field at Busch Stadium as fans file past Buck's casket during a memorial service.

MOMENTS

By the thousands they came, most clad in red, many soaked to the skin as they quietly broiled in furnacelike Busch Stadium to say so long one last time to Jack Buck, the legendary broadcaster who somehow represented royalty and family to St. Louisans.

When they made it through the line to his closed casket, they genuflected, saluted, tipped caps and wept over Buck.

— Post-Dispatch story on the memorial service

Among the mourners at Busch Stadium is Dave Kane of New Berlin, Ill., who offered his respects to Jack Buck by saying, "The greatest tribute we could give him today would be to be a nice person."

Cardinals pitcher Darryl Kile warms up in the outfield on June 20, 2002, as the hearse carrying Jack Buck's casket leaves the field. Cardinals fans would be grieving Kile's death two days later.

MOMENTS

"Cardinals pitchers were shagging balls in the outfield during batting practice ... and the crowd started yelling, hoping a player would throw a ball to them. One player obliged — he tossed the ball to a young boy who was only 3 or 4. It was so cool seeing the kid's eyes light up; even the player was smiling.

"The kid's father asked the player if he would sign the ball. Not only did he sign it, he took it to other players and got them to sign it, too. Watching Darryl Kile do all this, I couldn't help but think what a good guy he was.

"When the tragic news came out one week later, I was overcome by sadness. But when I saw pictures of Kile's family, my thoughts went back to a week earlier. The kid in the bleachers who Kile gave the ball to probably reminded him of his own son."

— Jeff Parkison, Walnut Grove, Mo.

MOMENTS

"It was heart-wrenching. We watched our heroes and they were broken-hearted. They had pictures in the montage of Mike Matheny crying and it broke me up.

"With Jack Buck, it was more a celebration of his life. But there's not much to celebrate about a 33-year-old man losing his life and leaving three little babies. It's so hard to understand how it could happen."

— Cardinals fan Carol Hill, after watching a video tribute to Darryl Kile at Busch Stadium

Zach Cole, 9, and his cousin Josh Blight, 7, of Florissant, Mo., pay their respects to Darryl Kile during a moment of silence at the stadium.

RIGHT: As if to include Darryl Kile in the celebration of the Cardinals' 2002 Central Division championship, center fielder Jim Edmonds gives Kile's jersey a spray of champagne.

Busch welcomes Bush

April 5, 2004

"St. Louis is one of the great baseball cities in America. It was my honor to be able to witness that first-hand. I want to thank the fans for such a generous ovation.

"I've done a lot of exciting things since I've been the president, but standing out here in Busch Stadium is one of the most exciting ones."

— President George W. Bush

The offering was a bit high, a tad outside. But a generous home-plate umpire — depending on his politics — might have called it a strike. Regardless, President George W. Bush's fastball to Cardinals catcher Mike Matheny was certainly the most memorable pitch of opening day 2004. Bush became the first president to throw out a first pitch at Busch Stadium when he hit Matheny's mitt. With security tight and Secret Service agents planted throughout and on top of the stadium, the president hopped out of the Cardinals dugout wearing a bright red Cardinals warm-up jacket. The crowd cheered loudly, with only a smattering of boos, as Bush waved and walked to the mound. He wasted little time in firing the ceremonial pitch, then waved as he departed the field in short order. Perhaps the most excited person in the stadium was Cardinals bullpen catcher Jeff Murphy. He had the honor of warming up the commander-in-chief outside the Cardinals clubhouse before the big moment. Murphy reported Bush took about 10 warm-up tosses before taking the hill. "We started playing catch, and I'd back up a little more with each throw," Murphy said. "We talked some baseball. I asked him if he wanted me to go all the way back, and he did. He was throwing from the normal distance from mound to the plate. He was throwing good." Afterward, announcer Joe Buck briefly interviewed Bush. "I was a little shaky out there," the president said, acknowledging some opening-day jitters. But, he added, "It's fantastic. All the players were telling me what a great place this is to play. It's such an honor to throw out the first pitch with a storied franchise." Some of the 49,149 in attendance grumbled about the extra security procedures and logistical hassles caused by the presidential appearance. But Gary Peck of Belleville, Ill., was more than happy to put up with the inconvenience. "He's my president, and he's out here relating to the everyday people," Peck said. "It's about time we have a president here for a game. It makes me proud." ∎

President George W. Bush throws out the first pitch on opening day of the 2004 season.

Before leaving the field, President Bush greets Cardinals Hall of Famers Stan Musial (right), Ozzie Smith (center) and Lou Brock.

Busch's 40-year man

MOMENTS

"Here's Rolen. He could give the Cardinals the lead. The pitch to him. Swing! And get up, baby! Get up! Get up! Get up! Get up! HOME RUN! Rolen has just given the Cardinals a 4-2 lead. He smoked it!

"Listen, LIS-TEN to Cardinal Nation!"

— **Mike Shannon's call of Scott Rolen's decisive home run in Game 7 of the 2004 NL Championship Series**

Perhaps no other St. Louisan has ties to Busch Stadium as binding as Mike Shannon's. A product of CBC High School, Shannon worked at the stadium for all of its 40 seasons, first as a player, then as a front-office employee, then as a Cardinals broadcaster. Shannon delivered the first Cardinals hit in the ballpark's inaugural game May 12, 1966. The following day, he hit the home team's first home run. In 1967 and 1968, he had the thrill of playing in a World Series in his hometown. "There's just no way to describe what that feels like," Shannon said. "I'd say it's a dream come true, but you can't even dream that. It's every superlative you can think of, and then some." Shannon's playing career was cut short by a kidney disorder, which forced him to retire after the 1970 season at age 31. The following year, the Cardinals hired him as an assistant director of promotion and sales. He left that position in 1972 to join Jack Buck on the play-by-play broadcast team and became a fixture in the second-level booth behind home plate.

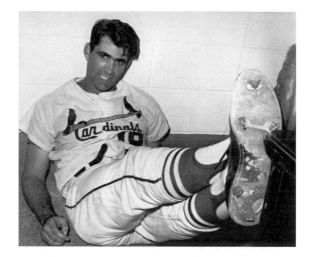

Mike Shannon relaxes in the Cardinals' clubhouse after contributing a home run in a 5-2 victory over Boston in Game 3 of the 1967 World Series.

Buck once said of Shannon: "He has that player's attitude, which I still don't have, where he can shake off a bad play or a loss by the next day. And I could be in the game 50 years and still not know some of what he does because I didn't play the game in the big leagues." Shannon has endeared himself to listeners with that unique perspective, his homespun values and colorful, if sometimes unorthodox, descriptions. Over the years, these analogies have become affectionately known as Shannonisms. ("This game began as a tiny worm and is blossoming into a large cobra.") Equally memorable are Shannon's signature calls of "Ol' Abner has done it again" and "swing and a long one ... get up, baby! Get up!" When the Cardinals move into the new Busch Stadium, Shannon will be celebrating his 35th season of broadcasting Cardinals games. ■

In a 1969 game at Busch Stadium, third baseman Mike Shannon is in the middle of a bizarre play at second base, where he puts the tag on the Dodgers' Bill Sudakis. Umpire John Kibler rules out while umpire Ed Vargo rules safe (Kibler's call eventually prevails). Shannon was covering second as Sudakis tried to stretch a bloop hit to center into a double.

MOMENTS

"This is a phenomenal seat. I've interviewed presidents up here. I've interviewed little kids that have come up in the booth and were only going to live two more months. I'll never forget the young man who had cystic fibrosis. A foul ball hit the guide wire. Hit here in the booth. Bounced up there. It hit like six different things and it landed right in front of this boy. He had a hot dog box — we had gotten him some hot dogs — and that ball landed right in that box. Right in front of him. He simply picked it up and ...

"You know, that kid died a month later. I can see the look on his face still."

— **Cardinals broadcaster Mike Shannon**

Mike Shannon enjoys a laugh with Jack Buck in 1985. Shannon and Buck shared the same booth at the stadium for 31 seasons.

Fellow broadcaster Dan McLaughlin takes a peek at Mike Shannon before a 2005 game. Bob Costas says of Shannon: "Not only is he quirky and therefore endearing and amusing, but he is — especially since Jack's death — what the Cardinals sound like."

Farewell to an old friend

Summer 2005

MOMENTS

"As you can imagine, I am somewhat disappointed to see it go. (But) the original Busch Stadium was built for another era: one that required a dual-use facility. I feel that today's design better accommodates its sole purpose: baseball. After all, from a business perspective, the object is to earn more money. Among other issues, the new seating arrangements allow for the owners to accomplish this objective."

— I.E. Millstone, founder of the construction company that helped build Busch Stadium

Fans attending Cardinals games during Busch Stadium's final season got a chance to say good-bye to an old friend and a chance to say hello to a new one. Which sentiment was more invigorating is hard to say. Giving their old ballpark a proper burial, the Cardinals chased one more pennant in 2005. All the while, an impressive new playpen took shape next door. By October, the future Busch Stadium — 1.3 million square feet in size and $398 million in price — was moving rapidly toward completion and a 2006 unveiling. An architectural complement to the surrounding buildings and warehouses, the red-brick beauty encroached on the south side of its predecessor, providing fans with an aesthetic preview of things to come. All that awaited the final stages of construction was the demolition of the still-occupied Busch. As if to show the new kid on the block how it's done, old Busch gave St. Louis one more memorable summer, a season that was in no hurry to end. A record flow of more than 3.5 million attended the season-long party as America's "best baseball fans" gave their departing ballpark a group hug. In the midst of the fun, the stadium's final days were ceremoniously marked with a "countdown" on the right-field wall. At each game, the descending number was pulled off by a notable figure from the past. From Larry Wilson to Stan Musial to Ozzie Smith, all the bases were covered. Hopes were high that the farewell party would last through a World Series. But the sentimental journey ended on Oct. 19, 2005, with a loss to Houston in the NLCS. A team going to its first Fall Classic celebrated on a field that had seen six World Series in 40 seasons. Afterward, thousands from the crowd of 52,438 lingered in the stands, applauding the winners, chanting for the Cardinals and cherishing Busch Stadium's final moments. ■

Ozzie Smith removes the final number in the countdown to the stadium's last regular-season game.

Ironworkers get a bird's-eye view of the old and new stadiums as they check a section of lights that had just been installed.

MOMENTS

"It's not necessarily the physical thing sitting here that matters to people. The memories are strong forever. And the other thing that's nice for people who are nostalgic about Busch Stadium is that we're on the same site and it's the same name. We will honor the tradition of Busch Stadium in the new Busch Stadium."

— Bill DeWitt III, Cardinals vice president for development

Watching a 2005 Cardinals road game on a video screen while camping out at the stadium is a midsummer night's dream for Matt Mueller of St. Louis and Casey Rallo of Wildwood, Mo. They had met at Busch three years earlier.

Debra Stolle of Chesterfield, Mo., lets her spirituality flow in a dance on Global Day of Prayer at the stadium in May 2005. About 3,000 Christians attended.

The terrace seats in center field provide a perfect vantage point for 18-year-old Marty Winkler of Oakville, Mo., to watch his favorite player, Jim Edmonds.

Little leaguers get a taste of the big leagues when they're allowed to parade around the field's perimeter before a Cardinals game on May 25, 2005.

MOMENTS

"Fans come to Busch for two main reasons: if the team is doing well and if the weather is good. We have no control over these factors.

"But if fans come to games and they like Ernie Hays' music, or they go home saying the hot dogs were hot, the beer was cold, and they got to see Fredbird, maybe they'll come back again."

— **Cardinals Vice President Marty Hendin**

A behind-the-scenes fixture at Busch Stadium since 1971, organist Ernie Hays communicates musically with the fans.

RIGHT: On a bittersweet day at the stadium, Reggie Sanders and the Cardinals take the field Oct. 2, 2005, for the final regular-season game at Busch.

MOMENTS

"The history and the tradition here isn't in the essence of the building as much as it is in the people who made it that way.

"It's not so much Busch Stadium itself. ... Take this show anywhere and people will cling to it just because of the history."

— **Former Cardinal Todd Worrell**

Fellow Hall of Famers Bob Gibson, Lou Brock and Ozzie Smith join in the applause for Red Schoendienst in a ceremony after the final regular-season game at the stadium.

MOMENTS

"I waited 10 years to see those Clydesdales. I signed to manage here when Anheuser-Busch owned the team, and I thought I'd see those Clydesdales all the time. But the brewery sold the team, and the Clydesdales never came.

"But I saw them today. They're beautiful. It was a thrill to finally see them on the field. I tried to get the Dalmatian to look at me, but he kept ignoring me. He must not like me."

— Tony La Russa, on the celebration following the final regular-season game at Busch.

The Cardinals' final regular-season game at the stadium on Oct. 2 is a day for nostalgia as the team honors many of the greats who played at Busch. "I've cried all week," says Angela Harrison of O'Fallon, Mo. "And when I go home and show my daughter my ticket stub, I'll start crying all over again."

Cardinals catcher Yadier Molina sits outside the dugout after making the final out of the NLCS — an out that sent Houston to the World Series and closed the book on 40 seasons of baseball at Busch Stadium.

The Cardinals' loss to Houston and the farewell to a stadium weigh heavily on the mind of Redbirds fan Dawn Perkins of Steelville, Mo.

MOMENTS

"When you grow up and you come here, it's so magical and you're running and your dad's telling you 'slow down, slow down,' but you want to run from the car, run from the garage and get up here and get your free hat or get your free helmet and see the Cardinals. And you want them to win so bad.

"To me, it's always been my favorite place, my favorite place in the entire world."

— Cardinals fan Paul Turner, at Busch Stadium's final game

Some fans will bend over backward to take home a souvenir, while others simply bend over. Amy Storck of south St. Louis County, Jasen Best of Springfield, Ill., and Ryan Grimaud of Glen Carbon, Ill., scoop up dirt to take home after the final game of the NLCS.

Talk about a Kodak moment. . . . After the last out in Busch Stadium's final game, fans capture the occasion with their cameras. From left are Jim Konersmann of High Ridge, Mo.; Haley Medvick of St. Louis; Clayton Cummings of Clayton, Mo.; and Celeste Capers of St. Louis.

MOMENTS

These were the typical faces of the Redbirds' expansive Midwestern empire; anxious young faces and sentimental old ones dressed in varying shades of scarlet and white, each one quietly treating this old gray lady like some precious touchstone.

They scribbled little love letters on every precious inch of Busch's pillars and walls. Others simply lingered around, reverently touching the walls, caressing the statues.

Busch Stadium's doors were about to close forever, but not before this heartbroken crowd washed it thoroughly with a proper mix of tears and cheers.

— Columnist Bryan Burwell, writing for the Post-Dispatch on Oct. 19, 2005

Ruth Burton embraces Quintin Washington as fans reluctantly leave Busch Stadium for the last time.

MOMENTS

"And so we arrive at the end of a 40-year journey. As we close the book on these memories, it is time to say good night and goodbye from the ballpark."

— John Ulett, public address announcer at Busch Stadium, signing off at 10:38 p.m. on Oct. 19, 2005

Disappointed that he couldn't get tickets to what proved to be the final game at Busch, Paul Wibbenmeyer waits nearly until midnight to hoist himself onto a banner pole and then over a railing to take photos of a nearly empty stadium.

217

Post-Dispatch sports columnist Bernie Miklasz, in the press box for Busch Stadium's final game.

From the sidewalk or roadways, Busch Stadium was never much to look at. It was an unimaginative concrete bowl, plopped down on a convenient piece of real estate. Build it and they will come ... spend money.

Busch was the product of an assembly line of multipurpose stadiums that sprouted across the nation in municipalities that sought to provide shelter for football and baseball teams in one no-frills space. Busch was never a homey or particularly inviting place. A neighborhood never formed around it. Quite the opposite, actually. It was built for expedience, flanked by on-ramps to whisk customers back to the suburbs as quickly as possible.

Some critics despised it. In a 1990 interview with the Post-Dispatch,

political commentator and noted Cubs fan George Will posed this caustic question: "'How did such a great and serious baseball town build such a hideous stadium?"

C'mon, now. Poor Busch Stadium couldn't help it. Busch was innocent, a victim of the times. Busch was caught between eras of baseball architecture. For pure baseball aesthetics, it could never rival the beautiful cathedral/ballparks that stood as monuments to the sport's heritage. Indeed, Busch's harsh look was softened by Edward Durell Stone's splendid arched top, an artistic marker that gave the structure a distinctive touch and a connection to the city's most recognizable landmark, the Gateway Arch. But for much of its existence, Busch had a synthetic feel, with its carpeted playing surface, man-eating mechanical tarp and symmetrical seating.

And that hot, hot heat. Baseball fans in St. Louis were tested like no others. If you had a ticket in the sections of Busch exposed to the direct sunlight during afternoon games, you prepared to suffer. If the weather was hot in St. Louis, it was 10 degrees hotter at Busch. (And if it was cold in St. Louis during the football season, it was 10 degrees colder at Busch.) That AstroTurf field was a Teflon frying pan, redirecting the heat back into the stands. Many years from now, scientists will conclude that global warming actually originated from the sizzling spot at 250 Stadium Plaza in St. Louis, Mo. At least the beer was cold.

Busch was practical and solid but could not exude the old-school charm of Sportsman's Park at Grand and Dodier. That was never the plan, or the point. In the early 1990s, we saw the advent of new stadiums built to look old, and Busch seemed even more outdated and out of place, a piece of baseball kitsch, held over from the 1960s and 1970s. Busch was a polyester leisure suit of a stadium in an increasingly hip and fashionable baseball culture. A mid-1990s interior makeover gave Busch some attractive retro styling, but it was merely a face-lift. This wasn't Camden Yards.

Fans head for home as the 2005 season winds down and the time to turn out the lights at old Busch draws near.

Harry Caray and Jack Buck, broadcasters who became synonymous with Cardinals baseball in different eras, have some fun before a game in 1982.

But we did not come here to condemn Busch. The wrecking ball took care of that.

And for a place so unappreciated for its sensible if sterile functionality, why did so many Cardinals fans get misty-eyed when the walls came tumbling down?

Well, Busch played a role in our lives in ways that had nothing to do with balls and strikes, line drives or pop flies, stolen bases or diving catches. Sure, the baseball was often special or spectacular. And despite the football Cardinals' chronic losing, the football Sundays weren't always bad, either.

Busch was the setting for World Series games played in three different decades. This was where Hall of Famers Bob Gibson, Lou Brock, Ozzie Smith, Red Schoendienst, Steve Carlton, Orlando Cepeda and Dennis Eckersley put on the Cardinals uniform. This was where Roger Maris concluded his career. This was where Mark McGwire broke the Maris single-season home run record.

This is where the young Albert Pujols put together the best first five seasons of any player in major league history, becoming to Busch what Stan Musial was to Sportsman's Park. This was where Schoendienst, Whitey Herzog and Tony La Russa assembled World Series teams. This was where Pro Football Hall of Famers Larry Wilson, Jackie Smith and Dan Dierdorf made their reputations. Pele was here. And the Beatles.

Upstairs in the booth was where Jack Buck supplied the baseball soundtrack for so many summers and gave us "That's a winner!" as a sendoff, launching all of those honking cars winding down the ramps at the parking garages next door.

This is where so many people came together to unify behind the shared love of Cardinals baseball. Men and women representing all races and ethnic groups and economic backgrounds, making the short drive from surrounding communities. And we welcomed visitors from all 50 states. These separate families that visited the ballpark dressed in red and became part of the extended family known as Cardinal Nation.

We spoke a universal language, in six simple words that required no translation: "Meet me at the Musial statue."

If you are reading this, chances are you were taken by the hand as a child and led into Busch for the first time by mom, dad or grandparent. And perhaps through the years, you perpetuated the cycle of our town's rich baseball life and guided your own kid or grandchild through those gates and into a whole new world.

Jordon Shaw, a 2-year-old from Highland, Ill., is ready to latch onto a home-run ball in a 1987 game at Busch.

Kristin Funk poses for her mother, Kay Funk, at the Stan Musial statue, a meeting place for generations of Cardinals fans.

The communal feel and family tradition is what made Busch Stadium so endearing. Busch provided precious scenes from our lives. I don't care how stressful the day's events were, there was something soothing about knowing you'd be heading to a Cardinals game later on, to kick back and enjoy the baseball and the company of friends or loved ones.

Other than the occasional snarling over inadequate pitching or a manager's perceived lunkheaded decision, Busch never contained the inherent hostility of Yankee Stadium, haughtiness of Fenway Park or the beer-garden frivolity of Wrigley Field. Visiting players knew that when they walked into Busch Stadium they'd be treated with courtesy by civil aficionados who knew the game and that fundamentally sound play would be appreciated. Busch Stadium led the majors in good manners for 40 consecutive seasons.

I can't think of a happier place for baseball.

During the final season, one of my favorite things to do after packing up the sportswriter's tools and leaving the press box was to roam through Busch and sit in different sections of the stadium. I'd sit alone in the still of the night, trying to absorb the magnitude of all that had transpired on these hallowed grounds. It was overwhelming, just thinking of those who passed through these gates, or climbed up the dugout steps, to mark the days and the years that made this the best baseball town in America.

The stadium lights were out, and the only sounds were made by the paper cups and the hot-dog wrappers blowing in the midnight wind. I cherished those few final moments inside this yard. It was difficult to believe that it all soon would be gone. The concrete disintegrated into dust, and even Stone's splendid scalloped arched canopy reduced to junkyard art. Material things can be destroyed, but no one ever will be able to remove the spirit that flowed through Busch, or haul away our memories.

Those who still recall a favorite image from a blissful afternoon spent at Sportsman's Park soon will be joined in this nostalgia by new generations of daydreamers who will allow their minds to wander back through time, to relive those hot summers at Busch.

Whenever an old stadium is abandoned, I believe it is mandatory that we send it off with some lyrics from Frank Sinatra's melancholy and moving song, "There Used to Be a Ballpark."

And the sky has got so cloudy
When it used to be so clear,
And the summer went so quickly this year.
Yes, there used to be a ballpark right here.

You know, Busch was a beautiful place after all.

Bernie Miklasz

There are Cardinals fans, and then there are Cardinals fans. Judy Green (left) high-fives Karen Shuford as Cookie Ray gets caught in the middle on April 8, 2005 — the final opening day at Busch Stadium.

CREDITS

Bill Martin takes down the Cardinals flags on the day after Busch Stadium's final game.

Cover photo by Dilip Vishwanat on Sept. 8, 1998 — the night Mark McGwire hit home run No. 62. **Text on back cover** excerpted from a Bernie Miklasz column on April 8, 2005. **Text for the inside flaps** of the book cover by Dan O'Neill of the Post-Dispatch. **Text for "Moments"** was compiled from Post-Dispatch readers' e-mails and letters; from Post-Dispatch interviews; and from the Post-Dispatch archives, unless otherwise indicated.